The Blessing of Favor

Experiencing God's Supernatural Influence

by

Kate McVeigh

Harrison House
Tulsa, Oklahoma

Read What These Christian Leaders Are Saying About Kate McVeigh

"Kate McVeigh is a bright young woman diligently fulfilling God's purpose and call on her life by reaching as many people as possible for the Lord Jesus Christ. We support Kate's radio ministry with our prayers and finances on a monthly basis because we have seen her heart and believe in what she is doing."

Dave and Joyce Meyer
Joyce Meyer Ministries
Fenton, Missouri

"I know Kate to be a dedicated and talented minister of the Gospel. She has a desire to reach the lost for Jesus Christ and to help encourage believers in their daily Christian walk.

"I am proud of her ministerial accomplishments and am excited about her new book."

Kenneth Hagin Jr.
Pastor/Executive Vice President
RHEMA Bible Church
RHEMA Bible Training Center
Kenneth Hagin Ministries

Contents

Introduction

The blessing of God's favor in your life is not based upon your background, talents, abilities, or anything you have earned. It is promised to you in the Bible, and all you have to do is believe it. Uncommon favor is available to every born-again child of God.

In this book I want to show you how the favor of God changed my life and the lives of others and how it can change your life too.

I have literally received hundreds of testimonies from around the world that tell how this teaching has changed people's lives: Lawsuits have been dropped, cases thrown out of court, raises and promotions given, relationships restored, and businesses reaching new levels of success.

My prayer is that you will grab hold of this truth and be transformed by the favor of God in every area. As you read this book, get ready to triumph and see uncommon favor explode on the scene of your life!

1

God's Favor Changed Me

But God, who is rich in mercy, for his great love wherewith he loved us,

Even when we were dead in sins, hath quickened us together with Christ, (by grace ye are saved).

EPHESIANS 2:4,5

1

God's Favor Changed Me

I held back the tears and ran into the house to escape. Alone, I let the tears flow as I cried out, "God, if You don't do something fast, I'm going to kill myself." I was fifteen years old the day I opened my new yearbook and read the stinging words, "Voted least likely to succeed—Kate McVeigh." I expected the best slogans to go to the popular crowd, but I didn't expect to see my own name attached to such devastating words. As a teenager, I felt no one liked me. This blow to my self-esteem confirmed it.

From the fifth grade, I had been in classes for slow learners. The other kids made fun of me. To them, I was the "dumb girl" who didn't fit in. When kids teased me and called me names, I would hold back the tears until I got home, where I could let them flow freely in the privacy of my own bedroom.

I would hide in the school bathroom each morning until the other students were in their classes so they would not see me walk to my Special Education class.

I developed an overwhelming inferiority complex. I imagined myself a hopeless loser and secretly wondered if my family knew there was something wrong with me mentally and kept it hidden from me. I even asked my sister, Helen, if I was mentally handicapped. I sincerely believed my family and friends refused to tell me the truth because they didn't want to hurt my feelings.

I expected rejection and regularly received it. I loved to play basketball, but my teammates were really mean to me. They used to call me "stupid" and "retarded." I was nicknamed "Sped" because I was enrolled in Special Education. My self-esteem was so low that I often wanted to commit suicide. After reading the revelation in my yearbook, I cried out to God, and He heard me.

My mother wanted to rip the words printed in my yearbook from my heart and mind as she listened to me cry into my pillow that afternoon. She was familiar with emotional and physical pain. Her mother had died when she was seven years old, and her father battled alcoholism. She had been taught by the devil's lie that illness was the will of God. She was born with curvature of the spine and suffered incredible pain as vertebrae in her back collapsed. For fifteen years she had ulcers in her stomach and believed if suffering was a virtue, then she was a godly woman. Despite what she was battling, she felt that her pain was no match for what I had experienced at the hand of my classmates that day.

I fell asleep that night with thoughts of suicide, while my mother prayed for God to help me. I knew there was a God, but I didn't have a personal relationship with Him. That began to change in 1984, when my uncle sent my mother some books and cassette teaching tapes from some anointed men and women of God. Listening to those teachings, my mother discovered salvation and gave her heart to Jesus. She also found God's goodness and understood that God wanted her well. She learned that God is a good God, and sickness is from the devil.

Transformed by God's Power

Although I didn't know it at the time, God was already working behind the scenes. My cousin, a born-again, Spirit-filled RHEMA Bible Training Center graduate, had shared the news of God's goodness and His power to heal with my mother. Because my mother had endured years of chronic back pain and the doctors had given up on her, my cousin talked her into flying all the way to Oklahoma to attend RHEMA's Healing School.

At Healing School, my mother received the baptism of the Holy Spirit and continued to learn biblical principles of standing in faith for her healing. She returned home and spent hours renewing her mind to the Word of God through prayer and study of God's Word. She then took what she learned and applied faith to her physical condition.

I repeatedly watched my mother as she refused to give in to the pain and the devil's lie. She had a crushed vertebra and missing disks beyond surgical repair. But after nine months of feeding on God's Word, she woke up one morning and she was completely healed. All the pain was gone!

My mother's healing had a tremendous impact on my spiritual life. I believe it was the catalyst that allowed the miracle of transformation in my own life. Not long after that, Mother invited me to attend Brother Kenneth E. Hagin's crusade in our hometown of Detroit, Michigan. The services were unlike anything I had ever experienced. I had never seen anybody raise their hands and praise the Lord that way in church.

Brother Hagin's message offered something completely new to me—hope. Although I was too intimidated to respond to his invitation to come forward that first night, the Holy Spirit kept drawing me. Brother Hagin's words burned hope into my heart, where before there had only been disappointment and despair. He prayed a prayer that evening, saying, "Lord, if there are those here tonight who don't know You, I pray that they won't be able to eat, sleep, or find any rest until they make Jesus their Lord and Savior.

Tossing and turning, I lay awake all that night thinking, *Why didn't I go forward to get saved this evening? What if I die tonight and go to hell before I accept Jesus as my Savior?* The next morning I promised myself I would find a way to the meeting that night, and when Brother Hagin gave the altar call, I would go forward.

I did exactly that. I went forward with many others and confessed Jesus Christ as my Lord and Savior. Brother Hagin laid hands on me, and I was filled with the Holy Spirit. A great weight lifted off my shoulders. Depression and fear, which had been my constant companions for so long, were gone. The thoughts of suicide were gone. I was free. My life was changed.

Favor Heals Insecurities

As "a new creature" in Christ (2 Cor. 5:17), I was no longer the "dumb, slow learner." The internal change began to be seen externally. Something on the inside was definitely working on the outside! I began to apply the principles of faith and confession I had heard, and I spent hours listening to tapes, poring over my Bible and confessing "I have the mind of Christ. (1 Cor. 2:16.) The greater One lives in me. Greater is He who's in me than he that is in the world." (1 John 4:4.)

I was amazed at my new ability to comprehend everything I read. Before my salvation, I had never completed an entire book from front to back. Soon after my salvation, I began reading faith-filled books and couldn't put them down because I was so excited about what I was reading.

I began to realize how God's love and favor could heal the insecurities in my life. I discovered my heavenly Father had poured His love, abundant blessing, and divine favor upon me because I had become His very own dearly beloved child. (Ps. 5:12; Eph. 2:4.)

After receiving Jesus, I was blessed to find a good Bible-believing church. My pastor preached on the subject of God's favor and continually taught us to claim favor in every area of life. He related how he daily walked in favor, showing us that favor was a gift from God; therefore, we should not expect rejection. He showed us practical applications as examples, such as finding the best parking spaces and purchasing items on sale.

He believed for favor with his church members and that they would want to be in the "helps" ministry. He expected a high percentage of the congregation to be tithers because he claimed favor with the people and believed they would tithe.

He taught us that if a raise was going to be given on the job, we should believe it would be given to us. God's favor would influence others on our behalf. If a good deal was to be found, we would find it. God would change impossible situations facing us. We discovered we could have favor with our teachers, families, friends, bosses, and other business contacts.

I began to confess that I had favor with my teachers, friends, and family. I started each day by saying, "Lord, I thank You that I have favor with You and man. People go out of their way to bless me and to do good to me today." I meditated on Psalm 5:12 NKJV:

> For You, O Lord, will bless the righteous; with favor You will surround him as with a shield.

Every day I continued to believe God in spite of my feelings. I refused to think or speak about myself opposite of who the Word of God said I was.

Two months after I received the Lord, the new school year began. I continued to put the Word to work in my life. On the outside everything seemed the same that first day. I returned to the same Special Education classes and practiced with the same basketball team. I knew on the inside I had changed, and it didn't take long for people to notice.

My teachers were shocked by my academic performance. Concepts that confused and frustrated me before now seemed simple to understand. People were noticing such a difference in me that they asked me what happened, and I told them that Jesus changed my life.

I also began to claim favor with my basketball team. Our coach rarely allowed me to play because I was so timid and made mistakes. I was a good player, but no one on the team had seen that side of me. I played great at home with my brothers, but around girls at school, I was so insecure that my hands would shake, and when it came time to shoot the ball, I would freeze because I was so nervous.

Now I stopped looking at the old Kate—the one always rejected by the team. Instead, I began to see myself walking in God's favor. I had to choose to see myself the way God sees me.

I claimed favor with my coach and my teammates, that I was no longer timid but confident because God's favor was working on my behalf.

I did this during my entire summer vacation, and when I returned to school, I was a new person. My coach and team-mates saw the formerly shy, timid Kate transformed. I had confidence in Jesus and was now able to concentrate. My natural athletic ability became evident. I was taken off the bench and put into games, voted "Most Valuable Player," and recognized as one of the top basketball players on my high school team.

Called To Preach

I immediately sensed a purpose for my life once I was born again. I knew I was called to preach. I was only sixteen years old, but I knew God had a plan for my life that included ministry.

I was not sure what to do about this "call," so I approached someone whose opinion I highly esteemed and was told that God could never use me to preach. Wow! What a let down! I was so tempted to be discouraged. But suddenly I felt strength on the inside and thought, *No, I know what God is saying to me, and I'm not going to get discouraged! I can do all things through Christ who strengthens me.* (Phil. 4:13.)

Within weeks of my giving my life to the Lord, a businessman heard my testimony and invited me to preach at a drug and alcohol rehabilitation center chapel service. I accepted the invitation not realizing my first congregation would be four hundred drug addicts and alcoholics who were required to attend chapel if they wanted to eat.

I went to that meeting with no idea what I would preach about. I prayed all day in an effort to come up with a message. Nothing!

When I arrived, I told the Lord I knew I could share the Gospel if He helped me. I believed I was anointed to preach, and as I stepped up to the platform, the Lord spoke into my heart, *Kate, tell them what you know.*

I knew two things: First, God is a good God because He saved me and set me free; and second, anyone who doesn't serve Him is dumb. So I got up and preached a sermon called "God Is Good, and You Are Dumb." All I said for forty-five minutes was God is good, and if you don't serve Him, you are dumb!

The businessman who invited me to speak thought he had missed God on this one. After I finished my eloquent sermon, I gave what I call "a reverse altar call." I asked everyone in the audience to stand. I said, "Those of you who want to be dumb and go to hell, just go ahead and sit down. Those of you who want to make heaven your home, come on down to the front." Guess what? Not one of them sat down! More than four hundred drug addicts and alcoholics came forward that night, weeping and crying, and made Jesus the Lord of their lives.

After all those people got saved, the businessman who invited me adjusted his tie with a proud look on his face and said, "I told you I heard from God!" What a glorious evening!

Until that time I couldn't even give an oral book report without thinking I would pass out. Now I was preaching the Gospel with boldness. God's favor changed everything!

When I began my junior year of high school, I didn't know one Christian. I decided to make some Christians myself by preaching the Gospel and leading people to Jesus. I reversed the peer pressure principle. If someone asked me with disdain, "Do you actually go to church?" I answered, "You mean you don't? What's wrong with you? You aren't filled with the Holy Spirit? Don't you speak in tongues? Man, you're strange! I'm the one who is normal. You're weird."

Throughout the school year, this approach allowed me to lead many teenagers to the Lord, including several teammates from my basketball team. Other students looked to me as a spiritual leader, and I was able to help many come to know the Lord as they saw the dramatic changes in my life.

My lifeline, the Word of God, was as important as the air I breathed. The years of pain and hopelessness were far from the freedom and joy I now experienced.

I completely reentered mainstream classes by the end of my junior year. I continued to experience increase in my life as I grew in my relationship with the Lord. My last year of high school consisted of excellent grades, many friends who liked and respected me, and record-breaking achievements in sports. Our basketball team won first place in conference that year.

Following high school I immediately moved to Oklahoma and attended RHEMA Bible Training Center. By faith, I studied and graduated and then entered the full-time ministry.

I want to encourage you as you read this book to see who you really are in Christ. In Him, you are more than a conqueror (Rom. 8:37), deeply loved (John 3:16; Eph. 2:4), accepted by God (Eph. 1:6), and made righteous through the blood of Jesus. (2 Cor. 5:21.)

When you *expect* God's favor to be demonstrated toward you, you will receive it in abundance. God's favor will pave the way to make your dreams come true.

2

What Is Divine Favor?

For he hath made him to be sin for us, who knew no sin; that we might be made the righteousness of God in him.

2 CORINTHIANS 5:21

2

What Is Divine Favor?

The Bible tells us in 2 Corinthians 5:21 that because of Jesus' sacrifice we have been "made the righteousness of God in him." If you are a born-again child of God, this Scripture is talking about you. Through the blood of Jesus, we are made right with God—the barrier and separation that once existed because of sin are gone, and we obtain right standing with our heavenly Father.

You are God's favorite child. This revelation transformed my life. I have so much favor operating in my life now that I believe I'm God's favorite child. When His favor begins to manifest and you see Him do so many good things in your life, you can't help but believe that you must be His absolute favorite child. (Deut. 32:9,10; Matt. 7:11.)

I believe that one day of favor is worth a thousand days of labor. God can do for you in one day what could take years to accomplish alone.

Psalm 5:12 says, "For thou, Lord, wilt bless the righteous; with favour wilt thou compass him as with a shield." Notice it says the Lord will bless us, the righteous, with favor. We must depend upon the Lord to see the favor of God come to pass in our lives. The more we acknowledge God's favor, the more we're going to see it in our lives.

When the Bible declares that the Lord will bless "the righteous" with favor, it's talking about you and me, because we are the righteousness of God in Christ. (2 Cor. 5:17.)

In Webster's dictionary, the definition of favor includes "...(1) friendly or kind regard; good will; approval; liking (2) unfair partiality; favoritism...attractiveness...be partial to; prefer unfairly...help; assist...to do a kindness for...endorsing...."[1]

To be *favored* means "(1) regarded or treated with favor; specif., (a) provided with advantages...specially privileged...."[2]

God wants to give you special privileges. The favor of God causes people to go out of their way to bless you without knowing why.

I don't know about you, but I really appreciate the *little* things that God does in my life. I always pray for favor everywhere I go.

One time I had preached in Italy and was returning to the States on an airline that I don't normally fly. I asked the Lord to bless me (and my friend who was with me) with an upgrade to first class because on the way there I had been uncomfortably squished between two people for ten hours, and I was exhausted when I arrived. So for the trip I said,

"Lord, You could upgrade us to first class. Thank You for giving us favor."

My friend said to me, "That's impossible because you are not a frequent flyer on this airline. They're not going to bump us to first class, especially going international."

I replied, "You don't know what the favor of God can do!"

At the airport the guy behind the counter told me I didn't have a seat on the airplane. Sometimes you pray for something, and it looks like the exact opposite is about to happen. I thought, *Yeah, that's because my seat is in first class. You just can't find it yet.*

Finally, they located seats for us in coach class, not sitting together and way in the very back of the plane. They were horrible seats! As he handed us our boarding passes, I was determined not to be moved by what I saw, so I just kept thanking God out loud for two first-class seats and confessing that He was going to do a miracle.

I was praying for two seats so that my friend would also receive the benefit of God's favor. I believe God wants to bless your life with so much favor that everyone around you receives the blessings of His favor as well. Each time my friend was tempted to say something negative, she stopped herself and just decided not to say anything, keeping herself in neutral. If you can't get in faith with someone about something, at least stay in neutral by keeping your mouth shut!

We went to board the plane. As my friend gave the attendant her ticket, she looked at me and was about to say, "See, it didn't work." Before she could say anything, I declared, "Don't say anything! It's not over yet." This is where a lot of Christians lose the battle. They receive a negative report and give up. But it's not over until God says it's over! Don't quit; play until you win.

As she went down the jet ramp, the attendant took my ticket, put it through the computer and said, "Wait, something's wrong with your ticket," and yelled for my friend to come back. That's when I got really excited. The attendant then informed us that we had both been upgraded to first class. My friend almost passed out! She said, "Kate, you really do walk in favor. It really does work!" I took the tickets and told my friend, "Follow me." Was it ever nice flying all the way home in first-class seats and drinking out of real glasses instead of plastic ones!

I told this story to one of my friends who flies overseas all the time. She said, "I cannot believe that you were bumped to first class. Do you know what a miracle that is?" She continued, "You just have enough guts to believe that God would bless you with that kind of favor."

God wants to bless all of His children with favor like that. We should believe God for favor on a daily basis. Many times the favor of God changes rules in your behalf. It causes people to go out of their way to bless you and is not dependent on whether someone likes you or not.

Every morning in the shower I confess favor. God will have you do certain things at certain times. For example, every time you vacuum you may pray in tongues. Maybe God will have you confess the Word over a specific area of your life each time you fold clothes or drive to work. Try to develop your own habit of confessing the favor of God.

When I pray for favor, I put it around my life. It surrounds me like a shield. (Ps. 5:12.) I thank God I have favor everywhere I go. I confess that people are going out of their way to bless me and to do good to me today.

Supernatural Favor

One of the first times I got to witness God's favor to others after I was saved was when my youth group went to a Christian concert. There were about five thousand people at the concert. Twenty-two kids from our youth group had decided to go with us at the last minute. We were running late and knew our chances of getting in were slim, so I said, "Let's claim favor for tickets and great seats." Then I made everybody pray. When we arrived, the concert was sold out.

We managed to get into the lobby area, but there were "Sold Out" signs everywhere, and the ushers wouldn't let any more people in. Our youth group said, "Let's leave," but I wouldn't budge. They asked me why I wouldn't leave with them, and I said, "Because I'm waiting."

"Waiting for what?" they asked.

"For the seats we prayed for!"

"But Kate, they're sold out."

Right about that time an usher came up to us and said, "Do you guys need seats?"

I said, "Yeah."

The usher said, "Follow me," and took us to this janitorial room and let us each grab our own chair. He allowed our whole group to put our chairs in front of the front row. We had the best seats in the whole house. We were the only ones allowed to do that. *God provided twenty-two extra front row seats.* Now that's favor!

God will create something for you if it's not there and needs to be. Remember, His supernatural favor in your life is not based on your background, looks, or personality. His favor is based on the Word of God and your belief that what it says about you is true. Favor can break through any barriers set before you. It is available to every child of God.

When you believe and activate your faith for God's favor, it will work for you. Someone may not particularly like you or your personality, but that doesn't matter. When you believe in God's ability to influence them, His favor on your life is supernatural. In other words, it supersedes natural circumstances.

Genesis 12:2 in *The Amplified Bible* says:

And I will make of you a great nation, and I will bless you [with abundant increase of favors] and make your name famous and distinguished, and you will be a blessing [dispensing good to others].

This Scripture clearly shows that God wants to bless you with supernatural favor. He wants you to be a blessing to everyone you meet.

We see this kind of favor in the life of Daniel. He and all the Israelites were prisoners in Babylon, but for reasons that can't be explained naturally, Daniel had favor with the leaders of the land.

> *Now God had brought Daniel into favour and tender love with the prince of the eunuchs.*
>
> DANIEL 1:9

In other accounts we learn that Daniel had so much favor with the leaders of the land that he was elevated to prestigious positions in the Babylonian kingdom.

Although the circumstances were stacked against him, Daniel eventually became the prime minister of Babylon. Good things happened to Daniel because of God's favor. Daniel loved and trusted God and expected things to turn out well for him.

Ephesians 6:24 NKJV verifies that there is special favor for those who sincerely love Jesus:

> *Grace [favor] be with all those who love our Lord Jesus Christ in sincerity.*

You can be just like Daniel. Call yourself a success. Expect promotion to come your way. See yourself highly favored, with good things happening in your behalf. Confess it daily. Believe for the impossible, and God's supernatural favor will work for you.

3

No More Curse

And if ye be Christ's, then are ye Abraham's seed, and heirs according to the promise.

GALATIANS 3:29

3

No More Curse

Galatians 3:13 says, "Christ hath redeemed us from the curse of the law...."

To learn what the curse of the Law is, we must go back to the first five books of the Bible, which are called the Pentateuch. The curse of the Law was basically threefold in nature: poverty, sickness, and spiritual death.

However, if you research a little further, you will see that there are many other things that fall under the curse of the Law. As you read Deuteronomy 28, verses 1-14 speak of the blessings, and the rest of the chapter basically speaks of the curse of the Law. Any time you read about the curse of the Law, keep in mind that you have been redeemed from it.

I like to read this passage of Scripture in *The Amplified Bible*, because it brings things out more clearly. Here are a few things in Deuteronomy 28 that we have been redeemed from.

> *Your ox shall be slain before your eyes, but you shall not eat of it; your donkey shall be violently taken away before your face and not be restored to you....*
>
> DEUTERONOMY 28:31 AMP

The Scripture says your donkey would be taken away from you. Your response may be, "Well, I don't have a donkey, so how does that apply to me?" In those times, a donkey was a form of transportation. In modern times, your car would be repossessed and not returned. That is a curse.

Not having enough money to pay bills is a curse. We've been redeemed from everything in this portion of Deuteronomy 28. As Christians, we grow in these truths, and the more we hear, the stronger we become.

Let's continue in verse 31. It says, "...your sheep shall be given to your enemies, and you shall have no one to help you." This Scripture is so good for churches. Lacking help is a part of the curse. I declare favor for my ministry by claiming there shall be helpers because I'm redeemed from not having help.

You can apply these principles in your life. Could you use help in some areas? Begin to speak it, and believe God for it.

Deuteronomy 28:38 AMP says, "You shall carry much seed out into the field and shall gather little in...." That means you will sow much but reap little. *A small and a slow harvest are a curse from which we are redeemed.* We have favor and blessing in every area of life.

The Bible illustrates the reaper overtaking the sower. (Amos 9:13.) We're living in that day and hour right now. Things are speeding up in the realm of the spirit. Things that normally would have taken a long time to come to pass are accelerating in the realm of the spirit. Our harvest is coming in quicker, and we will experience a quicker return in these last days because we are redeemed and can live in the favor of God.

When the sower goes out to harvest his crop, he has to do something to make it happen. He just doesn't cruise by the corn and say, "Hey, corn, jump in my wagon." In the same way, the harvest isn't just going to jump in your lap. You have to call it in by saying something. Give God words to work with.

The Bible says that the angels harken unto the voice of God's Word. (Ps. 103:20.) If we speak the Word, our angels will harken. If we're not speaking the Word, then they aren't harkening.

I believe that if you could look in the realm of the spirit and see angels, you would see that some of your angels are unemployed. Your angels should be saying, "I sure am busy. I'm busy making things happen because he's speaking the Word and calling for favor." Your angels should never be bored!

Deuteronomy 28:41 AMP says, "You shall beget sons and daughters but shall not enjoy them, for they shall go into captivity." Perhaps you are not enjoying your children because your children are not serving God. Stand on the Word of God, and call that child home. That's a part of our covenant, our inheritance. (Acts 20:32; Eph. 6:13.)

God is in the restoration business. The Bible says, "All your children shall be taught of the Lord, and great shall be the peace of your children." (Isa. 54:13 NKJV.) You can believe for your children to have great peace and be taught of the Lord. If they're not serving God at this moment, God can touch them right where they are and bring them home. God cares about everything that concerns you. He cares about what's in your heart.

Deuteronomy 28:44 AMP says, "He shall lend to you, but you shall not lend to him; he shall be the head, and you shall be the tail." God wants us in a position where we don't have to borrow. He wants us to reach the position where we become the lenders.

I heard one minister comment that the bank in his city approached him about borrowing some of his money because he had so much. Other banks were trying to convince him to put his money in their bank. He said, "Now they're wanting to borrow my money." Now that's being the head and not the tail.

Verse 50 tells us, "A nation of unyielding countenance who will not regard the person of the old or show favor to the young." Lack of honor in old age falls under the curse too. God wants you to experience honor. Lacking favor is a curse as well. Verse 59 says, "Then the Lord will bring upon [or allow in] you and your descendants extraordinary strokes and blows, great plagues of long continuance, and grievous sicknesses of long duration." You are redeemed from an extended healing process.

Maybe you have experienced chronic disease for years and it seems to be taking you forever to receive your healing. Notice that God said we've been redeemed of sickness and disease of a long continuance.

One of my board members who was saved, filled with the Holy Spirit, and on fire for God, was a diabetic for over forty years. Sometimes when we have had a disease for most of our life, it's easy to become used to it. We might not press in and apply our faith like we should because we've learned to live with it. God doesn't want you to live with sickness for the rest of your life.

My board member who was sick began to call "those things which be not as though they were." She called her body healed, but she still took her daily insulin shots and didn't throw her medicine away. She walked in wisdom, proclaiming, "The fact that I take medicine doesn't have to hinder my faith." Each time she took a shot it reminded her to say, "I'm healed." She'd pray repeatedly, "Father God, I thank You that I am *healed* by the stripes of Jesus, and I believe I am no longer a diabetic."

Then one day she woke up sick. Have you ever thought you were speaking the Word, and it looked like the opposite was happening? She was immediately rushed to the hospital. After a series of tests, the doctor told her, "Lady, the reason you are sick is that you are taking insulin for diabetics, and you are *not* a diabetic." She was healed by the power of God. She had lived with diabetes for forty years, and God wiped it out in a minute. She talked her way to healing.

It only takes one touch from God to change your life forever. We're redeemed from the curse of sickness.

God's Word promises no more curse. I believe that you and I need to make a decision and draw a line in the sand, so to speak, and say, "You know what, God? I'm not going to let the curse operate in my life anymore. I choose to believe Your Word." Then anytime the devil comes against you, you speak forth the Word of God, and you declare daily, "There shall be no more curse in my life."

We Have a Better Covenant

The psalmist David said, "The Lord is my shepherd; I shall not want" (Ps. 23:1), or "I shall not lack." We don't have to lack anything. You can lie down in bed at night and say, "Lord, I thank You that You're my Shepherd. I thank You that because You're the Good Shepherd, I don't lack for anything. God, I thank You that I don't lack wisdom." In fact, God said in His Word that if you lack wisdom, ask for it, and He'll give it to you freely. (James 1:5.)

You can say, "God, I thank You that I don't lack for good health, friends or money. I don't lack in any area of my life," because God is the Good Shepherd.

God's will for our life isn't that we barely get by. He's a God of supernatural increase. He's a God of abundance. And His plan for us is that we have *more* than enough. We need to tap into those things that belong to us.

Revelation 22:1-2 says, "And he shewed me a pure river of water of life, clear as crystal, proceeding out of the throne of God and of the Lamb. In the midst of the street of it, and on either side of the river, was there the tree of life, which bare twelve manner of fruits, and yielded her fruit every month: and the leaves of the tree were for the healing of the nations."

Verse 3 says, "And there shall be no more curse…." God is talking about you and me because the previous verse says, "… the leaves of the tree were for the healing of the nations." We need healing in our nation. Heaven doesn't need healing. God is talking about us on earth: "And there shall be no more curse…."

Galatians 3:13 is a very familiar Scripture. It says, "Christ hath redeemed us from the curse of the law, being made a curse for us: for it is written, Cursed is every one that hangeth on a tree."

Verse 14 continues, "That the blessing of Abraham might come on the Gentiles through Jesus Christ; that we might receive the promise of the Spirit through faith." We receive everything that belongs to us throughout the Word of God by faith.

The New Testament, or the new covenant, that we live under today is much better than the old covenant. It is similar to the difference between the ten dollar bill and the twenty. The twenty dollar bill has the ten in it, and then some. The difference between the old and the new covenant is the new covenant contains the old and then some.

Not only did God say that He'd remove sickness from the midst of us (Ex. 23:25), but we have the name of Jesus. It is the name that is above every name. (Phil. 2:9-11.) Those baptized in the Holy Spirit can pray in the Spirit. (Acts 2:4.) We have a better covenant because we have direct access to the throne room of God. (Heb. 4:16.) Hebrews 8:6 says we have a better covenant established upon better promises.

Faith is the source of the blessings of God that initiates the flow of favor. The Bible says, "…The just shall live by faith" (Rom. 1:17) and "We walk by faith, not by sight" (2 Cor. 5:7). The fact that you and I are redeemed from the curse of the Law, which shall be no more, must be received by faith.

"Me Too"

Look at Galatians 3:29. "And if ye be Christ's, then are ye Abraham's seed, and heirs according to the promise." If you've been born again and have received Jesus into your heart, then He's talking to you.

We belong to Jesus; therefore, everything that God promised Abraham He's also promised to you and me. In other words, you can study the Scriptures, and every time you see God's promise of something to Abraham, you can insert your name.

For example, in Genesis 12 when the Lord promised to bless Abraham, He said that He would bless him and make him a blessing. When you read that, you can shout *"Me too!"* because that includes you. When you read that God promised to make Abraham's name great, your name will be great as well. We can all be blessed and highly favored.

Jesus died on the cross to allow us to be redeemed from the curse, releasing us from poverty, sickness, and disease. *Redeemed* means "Ransomed…"[1] or "…to buy back…."[2] He bought us back with His very own blood. We can stand before God justified, just as if we'd never sinned.

If you are born again, that's the way that God sees you today. We are the righteousness of God in Christ. (2 Cor. 5:21.) Look at yourself through the blood of Jesus. You are never going to become any more righteous than you are right now, because Jesus made us righteous by His blood. (Rom. 5:9 AMP.) When we confess our sin, God is faithful and just to forgive us and cleanse us from all unrighteousness. (1 John 1:9.) You can stand before God, just as Jesus would stand before God, able to receive everything He's promised you, including the ability to walk in favor. As a matter of fact, the book of John says that God loves you as much as He loves Jesus!

The Bible tells us that when we are established in righteousness, oppression will be far from us. (Isa. 54:14.) When you realize who you are in Christ, oppression will have to leave. When you realize that Jesus bought and paid for your very life, it's impossible to stay discouraged. (1 Cor. 6:20.)

Every time you turn to the Word of God, you find God encouraging you. Even when you make a mistake, God's favor is there for you. He said, "And their sins and iniquities will I remember no more" (Heb. 10:17). When we make the decision to stand on the Word of God and declare by faith that there will be no more curse, we have exactly what we say.

Let's look again at some of the curses we've discussed and some others listed in Deuteronomy 28 AMP from which you and I have been redeemed. Meditate on these and say to yourself, "I have been redeemed from the curse of..."

- Poverty. (vv. 16, 18.)
- Confusion. (v. 20.)

- Sickness, such as allergies, fevers, and tumors. (vv. 22, 27.)

- Madness (losing your mind or having a nervous break-down), blindness (eye problems), or any kind of heart trouble. (v. 28.) Verse 61 also talks about all sickness and disease. That means we've been redeemed from every disease or sickness.

- Adultery. (v. 30.)

- My car being repossessed. (v. 31.)

- Lack of help. (v. 31.)

- My children going astray or not serving the Lord. (vv. 32, 41.)

- Reaping a small harvest. (v. 38.)

- Always having to borrow money. (v. 44.)

- Taking a long time to get healed—suffering from sickness for many years. (v. 59.)

- Not increasing. (v. 62.)

- Fear. (v. 66.)

- Not enough respect or favor. (v. 50.)

Maybe you have been experiencing a good amount of favor up to this point in your life. But are there areas where you have not seen favor? I'm sure there have been. This Scripture tells us that no more should we be lacking in favor in any area of our life!

I encourage you to keep pressing in for more of God's favor. Don't get discouraged if you don't see things changing immediately. Stick with it until you see God's favor manifest.

4

How To Activate
Favor in Your Life

For whoever finds me [wisdom] finds life and receives favor from the Lord.

PROVERBS 8:35 NIV

4

How To Activate Favor in Your Life

❦

Here are some ways to activate the favor of God.

1. Pray for Favor.

Even in little situations, God can work favor in your behalf. Have you ever had a time when maybe you talked to someone and what you said didn't come out the way you wanted it to? Maybe you tried to encourage someone, and by the time you finished, you thought, *I think I just discouraged them.*

I've learned that I can pray for favor in those situations. Maybe you were too busy and didn't have a chance to explain yourself to them. Instead of worrying about the situation, pray for favor. Pray God will give you favor with them, and they will believe the best of you. I've seen it work many times. The favor of God causes them to believe the best about me. They don't think much about my mistake. So if something didn't come out the way you wanted it to, pray for favor.

2. ACKNOWLEDGE FAVOR EVERY TIME SOMETHING GOOD HAPPENS TO YOU.

You acknowledge favor in your life by saying, "That's the favor of God" when something good happens. You will begin to experience more and more favor because what you respect will be drawn to you. What you respect is what you attract.

When you honor and acknowledge the favor of God working in your life, you'll experience increased favor. For example, every time you find a good parking spot, recognize it as the favor of God and thank Him for it.

3. AS WE BEGIN TO ACKNOWLEDGE AND RECOGNIZE FAVOR, WE WILL EXPERIENCE MORE OF IT.

Jesus walked in great favor and continually grew in it. I believe He had so much favor He practically had to insult Pilate to get Himself crucified.

Luke 2:52 says, "And Jesus increased in wisdom and stature, and in favour with God and man." Jesus increased in wisdom and stature, and He also increased in favor. The word "increase" means to grow, multiply, and enlarge.[1] Remember, the Bible said in Psalm 115:14, "The Lord shall increase you more and more, you and your children." I believe that we're going to see uncommon favor begin to manifest in our lives.

God's plan and will for your life is for you to increase in favor. We serve a God who is too much. Don't allow yourself to be comfortable with the little bit of favor you experience now; God has so much more. Ephesians 3:20 says that God is able to do exceeding, abundantly above all we ask or think! I have heard the word "exceeding" defined as "not enough room to hold." The Lord wants you to have so much favor that you don't have enough room for it all.

The psalmist said in Psalm 23:5 "…my cup runneth over." Our confession of faith should be that our cups run over with favor.

4. SOW FAVOR.

The Bible says in Galatians 6:7 that whatever you sow you will reap. In other words, if you sow favor into someone's life by showing them favor, you will reap favor in your own life.

If you want people to highly favor you, then you need to highly favor someone else. If you want someone to give you a chance at something, then you should give someone else a chance.

I remember one lady preacher who always gave me an opportunity. When I first started preaching, she would allow me to preach in her meetings and then recommend me to others. She is now reaping the seeds of favor that she sowed in my life. One of the ways she is reaping is that I became a monthly partner with her ministry. We should not forget the people who have shown favor to us and have helped us get started in certain areas.

God has blessed me with favor where my wardrobe is concerned. People are giving me clothes all the time! I believe it's because I've given a lot of clothes away. I have experienced Ephesians 3:20 NKJV, "exceedingly abundantly above," in my wardrobe. I don't have enough room to receive it all. Every closet in my house is stuffed full of clothes. In fact, just recently I went through my closet and gave even more clothing away. And guess what? Clothes just keep coming back!

Once I held a meeting and there was a couple in attendance who were just beginning their ministry. I thought, *I would like to sow a seed of favor,* and I had them preach. Then I received a special love offering for them. They were so blessed. I sowed into their lives and ministry. It's one of the reasons why I'm so blessed now. I receive hundreds of invitations to preach each year—so many that I can't get to all of them. That's what favor can do for you!

If we sow favor, we're going to reap favor in return. When you sow seeds of favor to someone else, you're going to open up the door to receive that favor in your own life. When you sow a seed in faith to God, that seed never leaves your life, just your hand. That seed will reenter your life when you need it most. It's coming back to you multiplied.

5. CONFESS FAVOR ON A DAILY BASIS.

You should confess favor every day of your life. Every single morning I get up and confess, "Lord, I thank You that I have favor with You and man today. I thank You, Lord, that people are going out of their way to bless me and do good to me today. I have favor everywhere I go."

You should continually speak the favor of God over your-self and your family. If you will confess the favor of God, stand fast for it, and refuse to be moved by what you see, hear, or feel, it will happen. The Bible says, "in due season we will reap, if we faint not" (Gal. 6:9).

You may even need to confess favor with your family members. I had to confess favor with my oldest brother. He was an alcoholic and not living for God. After I was saved, he would make fun of me. Every time I was around him, my brother would say sarcastically, "Praise the Lord, Kate." He would get right up in my face and tauntingly say, "Praise the Lord, Kate." I wanted to sock him and ask for forgiveness later.

Instead, I believed God for favor while my brother contin-ued to make fun of me. It didn't look like I had much favor with him, but I kept telling my brother, "Look, the Bible says in Acts 16:31 that if I believe on the Lord Jesus Christ, I'll be saved along with my household, so you might as well give up now. I believe I have favor with you. As a matter of fact, I call you saved, on fire for the Lord, and going to church."

That became my confession over my family—they are saved, on fire for the Lord, and going to church. I didn't want them just saved. I wanted them saved, on fire, and attending church.

Soon God put a really good Word church within walking distance from where my brother lived. Meanwhile, I contin-ued to confess, "I have favor with my brother, and God is opening his eyes." Some time went by, and then one day I received a telephone call from my brother while I was preaching in Kansas. He said, "Kate, you're not going to believe this. Do you remember that church you used to ask me to go to all the time?"

I replied, "Yeah."

He said, "You're going to find this hard to believe, but something woke me up this morning. All of a sudden I had this overwhelming thought, *You should go to church.* So I got up, got dressed, and went to church this morning, and I gave my life to the Lord."

Not long after that, he came to a service to hear me preach. He was standing next to me with his hands lifted in the air, praising God. Suddenly he stopped, nudged me, and said, "Praise the Lord, Kate!" Only this time he meant it. Now my brother tells me what to preach and is on fire for God.

You can activate the favor of God through confession. Speak it out just as you would any other promise in the Bible, just as you believe God for money or healing in your body. When you confess it, you release your faith. It's not enough to just have faith in your heart. You must release your faith.

One time I was watching a television interview of Brother Oral Roberts, and I'll never forget this man saying to him, "Brother Roberts, I've got a lot of faith."

He replied, "That's your problem. You've still got it. You've got to release it." What a powerful statement!

In order to see things happen in our life, we must release our faith. We have to turn our faith loose by the words of our mouth. Remember, the Bible says, "… let the weak say, I am strong." As you confess the Word of God and speak forth that Word, you're going to have what you say.

I travel all around the world preaching the Gospel and have believed that God would send people to minister to *my* family. I believe if you help take care of God's family, He'll take care of yours. I had been praying for my nephew to be saved, and one time while I was on the road, someone knocked on his door and began to witness to him. It was someone from my own home church, where I had preached many times. The person asked my nephew, "Are you saved?"

He replied, "I think so."

They answered, "Well, how do you know?"

He said, "My aunt saved me."

That wasn't good enough for them, thank God. They prayed with him there in his home and led him to the Lord! For years, I had sowed favor by leading other people's family members to the Lord. Remember, whenever you sow a seed into someone else's life, you will reap in your own.

6. Call your favor home.

I have a little dog named Favor. Favor is small, white, and fluffy. (Because of that name, my little niece thinks I wrote this book about my dog!)

Favor got out one day, and I opened the front door and called for Favor to come home. My neighbors probably thought, *Man, we knew she was one of those faith preachers, but this is going a little bit too far.* Favor was nowhere to be found. So I got in my car, and as I drove through the neighborhood, I called out the window for Favor. It wasn't long until Favor heard me calling and came running. I opened the car door, she jumped in, and I drove home.

The Lord spoke to my heart that day and said, *Just like you called your dog, Favor, home, you need to call your supernatural favor home.* Call the favor of God to operate in your life. Call your favor home. Call your blessings home. Call whatever you need—your money or healing—home.

If you will call those things which be not as though they were, you will have those things that you call for. (Rom. 4:17.) The word "call" in the Greek literally means "to…summon."[2] Have you ever been summoned to court? What does that mean? You have to show up. You must appear. You don't have a choice. When we start calling for the favor of God, it has to show up. It does not have a choice. It works the same in every area of your life. If you start calling for healing, healing has to come. If you call your body strong, it will become strong.

The Bible says to let the weak say they are strong. (Joel 3:10.) Let the poor say, "I am rich." (Matt. 5:3.) God told the weak person to say they're strong because they will have whatever they say.

7. EXPECT FAVOR

Several times in the Bible, Jesus told people, "According to your faith be it unto you." I often like to translate that as, "The sky is the limit." If you can believe it, you can receive it.

So you should be expecting the favor of God to explode on the scene of your life.

Have you ever seen someone with a rejection complex? They are always expecting people to reject them, and guess what? People do! Their own doubt and rejection draws that towards them like a magnet. Well, you can turn that around. Start expecting people to like you and favor you, and they will!

It's a matter of retraining yourself and changing the way you think. Continually remind yourself about who you are in Christ. Tell yourself, "The greater One lives in me" (1 John 4:4) and "I am accepted in the beloved." (Eph. 1:6.) Maybe you came from a background where you have experienced a tremendous amount of hurt and now have developed a rejection complex. Through the power of the Word of God, His favor can take the place of your rejection.

Make a conscious effort to think the best in every situation. For example, whenever I used to get a phone call from someone important, I would immediately think I did something wrong or it was bad news. Through the years I have retrained myself to think positively in those situations. Besides, they almost always turned out to be positive anyway—the devil was just lying to me! You can't let him do that to you! Just think of it this way: If it is bad news, your faith in God can turn it around anyway! Expect favor instead of rejection.

Here's a catchy acronym I came up with for the word favor:

Faith

Activates

Victorious

Outrageous

Results

5

Forgiveness Brings Favor

And whenever you stand praying, if you have anything against anyone, forgive him and let it drop (leave it, let it go), in order that your Father Who is in heaven may also forgive you your [own] failings and shortcomings and let them drop.

But if you do not forgive, neither will your Father in heaven forgive your failings and shortcomings.

MARK 11:25,26 AMP

5

Forgiveness Brings Favor

If we want to see God's favor in operation, we must walk in forgiveness. We can choose to hold grudges or choose to walk in love and forgiveness. I have a little saying that goes like this: When someone offends you, don't nurse it, don't rehearse it, but curse it, disperse it, and God will reverse it.

Forgiveness is not based on how we feel. Instead, it is based on our actions concerning what God's Word says. Just as we believe and pray for things by faith, we can forgive by faith.

When bitter thoughts arise, don't let your feelings dictate to you. Walk in love by faith, and the feelings will eventually line up. Jesus is a perfect example of a Man who walked in forgiveness. By doing so, He brought God's love to the lives of many people.

In Matthew 14 there is a beautiful story of forgiveness. John the Baptist, Jesus' best friend and cousin, was brutally murdered—beheaded by King Herod. When Jesus heard the news, He went away to be alone. Most of us, when we receive bad news, do not want to be bothered by people. We just want to be left alone.

Someone found out where Jesus went, and before long a great multitude followed, many of them sick. Instead of attacking Herod, Jesus attacked the devil by healing the sick. The scriptural way to overcome evil is to do good. For instance, Romans 12:21 NLT says, "Don't let evil get the best of you, but conquer evil by doing good." And Matthew 5:44 tells us to love our enemies, and pray for those who persecute us.

As Jesus walked in love and forgiveness, God showed His favor by pouring out His glory.

Choose To Forgive

When I first received Christ, I was on fire for God. I passed out tracts every day after school and developed a burning desire to see people saved. There was just one problem: a girl in my life who had been very mean to me.

Both the Lord and my mother spoke to me (the Lord spoke in my heart) about forgiving this girl. My mother would hang signs on my bedroom mirror reminding me to pray for her. It wasn't easy at first because my flesh would get in the way when I would pray. I thought that if I asked God to bless this girl, He just might do it. I needed to forgive.

Unfortunately, many of us short-circuit God's power and favor in our lives because we do not realize that a lack of forgiveness hurts *us* more than it hurts the person who wronged us.

Hurting people hurt people. If someone is hurting you, they may very well be hurt and miserable themselves. Romans 5:5 says, "...the love of God is shed abroad in our hearts...." We can see from this verse that love for those people already exists in your heart. You *do* love those people. They need your help and prayers.

I put my feelings aside, chose to act on God's Word and to pray for my enemies. It was not long before I really felt a love for this girl. Soon all the bitterness was gone.

One day when I was home, I heard a knock at the front door. The girl who had hated me for so long stood at the entrance. I could not believe my eyes. She told me she just happened to be in the area and wanted to stop by to ask me a question.

She said I had really changed since my salvation experience and wanted to know all about what happened to me. Forgiveness brought God's favor. As I shared the Gospel with her, she was born again and filled with the Holy Spirit.

She also told me that because of a problem in her knee, she might have to have an operation. We prayed together, and the power of God hit her so hard that she fell to the floor. When she arose, she was totally healed. Forgiveness brought His favor to my life. There are rewards for forgiveness.

There's a story in the book of Judges that tells how Jephthah's brothers held part of his money. He became angry, left, and later forgave them. In Judges 11:29 it says that the Spirit of the Lord came upon him. I believe the Spirit of the Lord came upon him as a result of his forgiving, and he received the blessing.

Forgiveness will cause good things to come into your life. I like to think of forgiveness as canceling a debt. If you forgive a debt, you may tear up the piece of paper showing the amount owed. You forgive the debt by wiping it out. Then the person doesn't owe you a dime. When I forgive someone, I draw a mental picture in my head and tear up the paper, saying, "God, I forgive them, and now I'm asking You to as well." Once I do that, they now owe me nothing. Not even an apology!

The Bible talks about the cancellation of someone's debt. (Matt. 18:21-35.) That offense or hurt needs to be cancelled. When we forgive, it opens the door of God's favor to flow freely in our life.

Joseph's Forgiveness Brought Favor

The life of Joseph found in the book of Genesis offers another good example of forgiveness bringing God's favor. Joseph had a great opportunity to walk in bitterness, but instead, he chose to pass that opportunity right on by.

Joseph's brothers were jealous of him because he was their father's favorite son. (Gen. 37:4.) Joseph wore a special coat of many colors that his father made for him. His brothers took the coat from Joseph, killed a goat, and put its blood on the garment to convince their father that Joseph was dead.

The brothers sold Joseph to the Ishmaelites for twenty pieces of silver. Those merchants took him to Egypt, where he served as a slave.

In Egypt, Joseph was lied about and thrown into prison for many years. (Gen. 39:17-20.) He plunged from the most highly favored member of Jacob's family to living in the lowest dungeon in a foreign land.

Under those circumstances, Joseph could have chosen to become bitter, not better. Without a doubt he could have become bitter toward his brothers, but instead he chose to please God and become better. Because Joseph forgave, God granted him great favor. He became the prison administrator (vv. 22,23), then was freed to become second in command of Egypt. (Gen. 41:40-44.)

Joseph's decision to forgive enabled God to bless him abundantly. It also released God's favor for many others. As the second highest ruler in the land, Joseph was able to bring his entire family out of severe drought into plenty. (Gen. 45:9,10.) He saved his ancestry and preserved his family line, from which Jesus was born. I'm glad that Joseph chose to forgive his brothers and activate God's favor.

God's favor will work for you as you believe and expect it in your life. Truths from God's Word will change your situation. Expect favor in your job, your business, your ministry, your family, and your social life. You will never be the same again.

You can walk in favor with God and man.

6
Favor in Relationships

And Jesus increased in wisdom and stature, and in favour with God and man.

LUKE 2:52

6

Favor in Relationships

We already know from Psalm 5:12 that we have favor with God, but we can also have favor with man. The word "man" in the above verse speaks of all mankind.[1] It includes your boss, family members, teachers, pastors, spouse, and others.

Before going into full-time ministry, I had problems with a moody woman at my job. One day she would be very nice to me; then the following day she would be really nasty. I never knew if she was going to blow up in my face or be nice to me. I felt as though I had to walk on eggshells when I worked near her.

Moody people are usually unhappy and take their frustrations out on the people around them. Often, they will try to control you with their moodiness.

It is important to realize that the person stirring up trouble is not the source; the devil is behind it. The enemy often works through people. In Matthew 16, Peter was used by the enemy when he said to the Lord, "Be it far from thee..." referring to going to the cross, and Jesus had to say, "Get thee behind me, Satan." Jesus recognized the source of the trouble that was coming against Him. He didn't say that Peter was the devil, but He recognized the source and spoke to it.

Even Christian people can be used unaware. But you can pray and take authority over any hindrances that would attempt to block your favor, and you can send love towards that person. In some situations, the Lord may even have that person leave if they will not change. He can move them out so that you still have favor. Pray for them and trust God. He works on your behalf. God can make a way where there is no way. (Isa. 42:16; 1 Cor. 10:13.)

I tried many different ways to solve the problem with the woman at my workplace. I tried being kind and sweet, but it seemed that when I did, she took even greater advantage of me. Then I decided I would be firm and not let her run over me, but that only made matters worse.

One day as I was praying for this woman and the situation, the Lord showed me that I could bind the spirit operating through her and claim favor with her. I needed to take care of this problem in the spirit realm, not in the flesh.

For we wrestle not against flesh and blood, but against principalities, against powers, against the rulers of the darkness of this world, against spiritual wickedness in high places.

EPHESIANS 6:12

Each day as I went to work, I continued to thank God, stand on the Word, and believe Him for favor in this situation.

After a couple of months, something happened. It seemed as though this woman had been transformed. Every day at work she would go out of her way to bless me and say kind things to me. Her response wasn't phony. To this day she is very kind and does things to help me in my ministry.

Favor in Your Marriage

The Word of God says that we can have favor with *all* people. "All people" includes your husband or wife. God desires that married partners grow in favor with one another. But to see God's favor in this area, you cannot be selfish. You must sow favor in order to reap it. (Gal. 6:7.)

Every married person can sow seeds of favor toward his or her spouse by walking in love and preferring the other person before themselves. The Bible instructs us to "walk in love, as Christ also has loved us" (Eph. 5:2 NKJV) and to be "kindly affectionate to one another with brotherly love, in honor giving preference to one another" (Rom. 12:10 NKJV).

Divorce would not be as rampant in the world today if husbands and wives were constantly trying to outdo one another in love. I know a pastor and his wife who are great examples of God's love. I have been around them a great deal. I can truly say they walk in love toward each other just as much outside the church as they do on Sunday mornings.

They continually seem to try to outdo one another in love. He loves her as Jesus loves the church. He treats her like a precious gem. He always opens her car door, helps wash the dishes and brings her a fresh cup of coffee in bed every morning. In return, she is always going out of her way to bake his favorite pie or to cook his favorite meal.

This couple testifies that at the beginning of their marriage they promised to love one another and to work through their problems together. They made a rule that the word "divorce" was never to be used in their relationship. After more than thirty years, they are still experiencing a happy and successful marriage based upon God's love. You, too, can have a successful marriage and see God's favor at work. Remember, you must sow favor in order to reap it.

Put Your Faith in God

When you walk in favor, you don't have to pressure people. Faith doesn't put pressure on people. Have you ever been with people who tell you how the Lord blessed them? For example, they pray next to someone saying, *I really like that ring. Lord Jesus, I wish I had one like the one she is wearing.* That person then hands the ring to them, and they happily report, "Look what God gave me."

In those cases, God didn't bless them with something. The giver was talked out of it. I like to see God move when I'm standing in faith for something and don't tell anyone. I don't tell anyone what I am believing for and don't let anyone know. Then when someone walks up to you and blesses you, you know God answered your prayer. It's a greater testimony when no one knew what you were believing for. Faith doesn't pressure people.

7

Favor for Finances

Beloved, I wish above all things that thou mayest prosper and be in health, even as thy soul prospereth.

3 JOHN 2

7

Favor for Finances

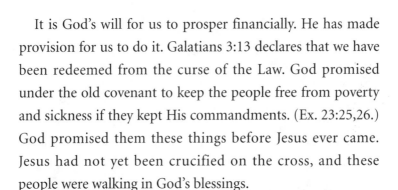

It is God's will for us to prosper financially. He has made provision for us to do it. Galatians 3:13 declares that we have been redeemed from the curse of the Law. God promised under the old covenant to keep the people free from poverty and sickness if they kept His commandments. (Ex. 23:25,26.) God promised them these things before Jesus ever came. Jesus had not yet been crucified on the cross, and these people were walking in God's blessings.

If God promised prosperity under the old covenant, think how much more we, as His children, can partake of all His goodness under the new, and better, covenant. (Heb. 8:6.)

You can prosper in finances through God's favor. The apostle Peter said in 2 Peter 1:2 AMP:

May grace (God's favor) and peace (which is perfect well-being, all necessary good, all spiritual prosperity, and freedom from fears and agitating passions and moral conflicts) be multiplied to you in [the full, personal, precise, and correct] knowledge of God and of Jesus our Lord.

Favor on the Job

You, as a believer, should not be moved according to the world's ways. For example, your company where you work may not give raises. This does not have to apply to you because as a Christian, you have favor with God and man.

I began expecting and experiencing God's favor in my finances when I was just a teenager. At that time I desperately needed a job that paid well, but some people told me I would never find a good job because in their opinion, no one would hire a person who had spent most of her life in Special Education classes.

Despite these negative reports, God was speaking to my heart and assuring me that His desire was for His children to have the very best. Immediately, I began to believe for favor to receive a good job with a good salary.

A friend then told me about a large company that was hiring. The only catch was that they were looking for experienced people. Never in their history had they hired anyone as young as I was.

On my way to the interview, I thanked God that I would have favor with every person in that place. At the interview they asked if I had any experience in the areas for which they were hiring. I told them I could learn fast and that I was the best person for the job. I assured them they would never find anyone as hardworking as me, despite my lack of experience.

Against their ordinary procedure, they hired me. It was a wonderful job with excellent benefits and a good pay scale. I discovered that as believers we can have favor in the workplace.

Your Perception

In the thirteenth chapter of Numbers, Moses sent twelve spies to check out the land that the Lord had promised the Israelites. The Bible says that all twelve of the spies saw the same thing—a land flowing with milk and honey and a land with rich soil, which produced huge, juicy grapes. They also saw some giants in the land. (v. 33.)

The Bible says that ten of the spies came back with an evil report. (v. 32.) They reported how difficult it would be to take the land with the giants living there. Only two returned with a good report, saying, "We are well able." Ten of them had faith in the giants; two had faith in God.

And they told him, and said, We came unto the land whither thou sentest us, and surely it floweth with milk and honey; and this is the fruit of it.

Nevertheless the people be strong that dwell in the land, and the cities are walled, and very great: and moreover we saw the children of Anak there.

NUMBERS 13:27,28

Numbers 13:30 says, "And Caleb stilled the people before Moses, and said, Let us go up at once, and possess it; for we are well able to overcome it."

Caleb had a faith report. He said, "We are well able," or "We can do this. If God is for us, who can be against us?" (Rom. 8:31.) Verse 33, says, "And there we saw the giants, the sons of Anak, which come of the giants: and we were in our own sight as grasshoppers, and so we were in their sight." Notice they said, "We were in our own sight as grasshoppers." They saw themselves as small. They saw themselves as little. They saw themselves as grasshoppers, and you know what? What they saw in themselves, others saw in them too.

What you perceive and believe of yourself is what others will think and believe about you. If you believe that you walk in favor, that God has blessed your life, and that you are anointed, then others will see you the way you see yourself.

Earlier I said that Jesus practically had to insult Pontius Pilate to get Himself crucified. Everywhere He went, crowds followed Him; but there was a time or two in His life when people came against Him.

There was a time the crowd wanted to throw Jesus off a cliff. (Luke 4:29.) The Bible says that Jesus walked right through the midst of them. (v. 30.) One translation says that He "slipped away through the crowd and left them." (NLT.)

I like that description. It reminds me of how a greased pig contest was described to me one time. You take a hog and grease it down with oil to make it slick. Then you let the hog go and try to catch it, which is almost impossible.

Jesus slipped right on through the crowd because He was slick—anointed. The word "anoint" means to pour on and to smear all over.[1] The Bible says you have been anointed with the burden-removing, yoke-destroying power of God. (Isa. 10:27.) Just think: You're anointed like a hog! Every time the devil throws something against you, you just slip right on through his plan. He may try one thing and then something else, but you continue to slip through to victory.

It's a Fixed Fight

Have you ever thought, *I don't know how God's going to bring me out this time?* Psalm 34:19 says, "Many are the afflictions of the righteous: but the Lord delivereth him out of them all."

The Bible also says that we are to "fight the good fight of faith." (1 Tim. 6:12.) The good news is this fight of faith is a fixed fight! It has already taken place, and Jesus won the battle for us. (Col. 2:15 AMP.)

You can rest in the midst of that trial you're going through and say, "Hey, I already know how I'm coming out of this, and I have total peace because Jesus has won it for me."

A good fight is one you win. One time I was getting ready to take a trip, so I turned on the TV while I was packing. A sportscaster was interviewing two boxers, and one said, "I want to give honor and glory to my Lord Jesus Christ." That immediately got my attention. Then they interviewed the next guy, and he said something like, "I'm gonna bust your head!"

Right then I knew God's man needed my prayers! I began to take this personally. It was like God versus the devil on live television. They started fighting, and I stopped everything I was doing and began to pray in the spirit. Sitting on the edge of my bed, I shouted, "Lord! Give him the strength of Samson! I pray You will anoint him to sock the daylights out of that guy!"

The announcers kept saying how close the fight was, and I prayed even more fervently. By this time I was really getting into it. Then suddenly around the fifth round these two announcers came on and interrupted the fight. They went on to tell what happened in the next round and the round after that. Then they told who won the fight. I found out I was watching a repeat! This fight had already taken place. Boy did I feel dumb!

Here I was praying like crazy, and this thing had already taken place. Right then it hit me how we as Christians are fighting the good fight of faith. No matter what you're going through, Jesus already won the battle for you! It's a fixed fight. You win!

After hearing that my guy won the fight, I sat back very calmly and watched the rest of the match. I already knew the outcome so it didn't matter what happened in that ring. My guy could have been knocked down for the count and it wouldn't move me. Why? Because I already knew the outcome. The same is true in what you are going through at this very moment. Jesus won the battle for you, so you can rest knowing no matter how hard the devil throws his punches, you're coming out of this in victory!

The Bible says, "We which have *believed* do enter into rest…" (Heb. 4:3). When you're resting, you're not fighting. After I knew that my side won the fight, I could sit back and not be stressed out over the outcome. You might not know how God is going to do it or whom He may use, but you can be sure that He'll deliver you "out of them all" just as we read in Psalm 34:19.

Let Go and Let God Do It

Have you ever hit a financial wall in your life, and you thought, *Now, Lord, I know so-and-so has a lot of money. I pray that you speak to them right now, God; speak thousands of dollars to them, Lord. Put it in their heart to help me financially?* God almost never does it the way you tell Him to.

God does not want your eyes on any person as your source. He wants you to see Him as your Source.

Have you ever tried to accomplish something in the flesh? It's bad news. Whatever you do in the flesh, you've got to keep in the flesh. (Rom. 7:5.) God promised Abraham and Sarah that they would have a child. (Gen. 15:4.) But they didn't see it happen right away. Sometimes when we don't see things happening right away, we try to do it on our own. We can't do it but must let God do it.

Sarah decided to take matters into her own hands. She sent her servant girl, Hagar, to Abraham, and the servant girl became pregnant. She had a son, Ishmael (Gen. 16:11), and they had nothing but trouble. Why? Because that wasn't God's way; it was their own plan.

What you produce in the flesh, you must keep in the flesh. If you try to earn favor in the flesh by doing your *own* thing without letting God do it His way, then you must live with the consequences.

It would have been better for Abraham and Sarah to wait for God's best than try to make something happen in the flesh. Thank God, He did eventually bring them Isaac, the son of promise. (Gen. 17:16-21), and they got on track with God's plan.

Have you ever felt as if you birthed an Ishmael in your life? Maybe you wanted something so bad you brought it to pass without waiting on God's best plan. I have gotten ahead of God and wished I could go back. Thank God, we can repent.

In other words, when it's God's will, it's His bill! What God orders, He pays for. When God does it for you, He will see it through. Let go and let God do it!

Favor for Promotion

A good friend shared this story with me a few years ago. He is a Christian man who began to learn about the favor of God. He began to claim favor on his job. In prayer, he asked for favor with his boss and everyone else he worked with, believing that God's divine favor was surrounding him as a shield.

One day his boss called him into his office and said, "We have never done this before, and this doesn't even make sense, but we're giving you a raise." As a result of that raise, this man ended up making more money than his boss did. The employer even told him, "You are the first person in the history of this company who has ever made more money than I have."

He testifies that this happened because he is a tither and a giver, and he believed God for favor.

Psalm 75:6-7 reminds us that promotion comes from God. We can rely on the favor of God to help us find good jobs and get raises and promotions.

When you are doing your best and meeting, or exceeding, the company's production standards, your boss will be pleased with you and approving of your work. You will be appreciated as a valuable employee. You may feel as though you are giving your all at your job but it is not noticed. I encourage you to trust God.

Begin to believe God's Word and what He says about His divine favor being bestowed upon you. Know that God has already set His affection upon you; He is pleased with you and will cause you to enjoy favor with the people in your workplace as well.

God's Favor Causes Rules To Change

I fly all over the United States to preach. There have been times when an emergency has arisen or revival has broken out in the church where I've been ministering, and I needed to stay longer.

Airline rules usually don't allow tickets to be changed without a fee, especially on short notice. One time in particular I called the airline and was told that my ticket could not be changed so that I could fly out several days later.

I prayed and asked God for favor. When I went to the airport to see about it, the person behind the counter said, "We normally don't do this, but we will change the ticket for you today."

My Aunt May has a great testimony of God's favor working on her behalf. As a widow, she got most of her income from Social Security. Several years ago she learned that the age for receiving Social Security benefits had been changed because of changes in government policy. That meant she would not receive any more checks until she was older. With six children, she desperately needed that money and didn't know how she would support herself without it.

We prayed and agreed for favor. One day, seemingly out of the blue, the Social Security office called to say that she would be receiving her checks again.

Not only was this call made on a Saturday (normally government employees don't work on Saturdays), but she was told, "Your Social Security benefits have been restored." God's favor even works on your behalf with the government!

8

Love Brings Favor

But the Lord was with Joseph and showed him mercy, and He gave him favor in the sight of the keeper of the prison.

And the keeper of the prison committed to Joseph's hand all the prisoners who were in the prison; whatever they did there, it was his doing.

The keeper of the prison did not look into anything that was under Joseph's authority, because the Lord was with him; and whatever he did, the Lord made it prosper.

GENESIS 39:21-23 NKJV

8

Love Brings Favor

Joseph's story found in Genesis 39 is an excellent example of how love brings favor when you exercise it in your life.

Joseph had done nothing wrong when he was thrown into prison. The wife of his master, Potiphar, had tried to seduce him, and when Joseph said no to her, Potiphar's wife became very angry. (Gen. 39:12-19.)

She decided to get even with Joseph by lying and falsely accusing him of attacking her. As a result, Joseph was thrown into prison. (Gen. 39:20.) It was unfair. Have you ever been accused of something unfairly? Even unfair accusations cannot keep God's favor from working for you.

God's favor continued to work on Joseph's behalf. We read in Scripture that even being in prison could not keep him down. Joseph had so much favor that the keeper of the prison put all his administrative work in Joseph's hands.

In the book of Genesis we see that Joseph operated in the favor of God. I believe Joseph caused the favor of God to come on the scene of his life because he walked in great love.

Joseph operated in love towards his brothers and others who had done him wrong.

God is calling the body of Christ to a greater level of love. God wants us to walk in a deeper walk of love. It's easy to walk in love when no one is home. It's when everyone shows up that it becomes a little bit more difficult. You really don't know if you're walking in love until you have the right opportunity.

I woke up one morning meditating on 1 Corinthians chapter 13 in *The Amplified Bible* version. I started confessing it about myself. I said, "I endure long. I am patient and kind. I'm not envious. I'm not jealous." That's putting the Word into your heart.

Then I got a phone call. One of my friends called me and said, "Kate, I have a story to tell you that's going to bless your socks off. There's a young girl who has been in the traveling ministry for only three months. She was preaching in a service with only fifteen people, and a woman in the service was so blessed by this young girl's ministry that she gave her a check for $1 million." After my friend finished, he asked, "Doesn't that bless you?"

I answered, "Praise the Lord, *I think.*"

Then he said, "The story gets even better. The next day the lady's mother flew in from out of town. She is twice as wealthy as the daughter, so the mother wrote the young girl a check for $2 million." He asked again, "Doesn't that bless you?"

I could feel my frustration starting to rise. This girl was walking in some favor! Suddenly the devil said, "Kate! You have spent nearly thirteen years in the ministry traveling and believing God to supply your needs. Look at that little whip-persnapper. She's only been in ministry for three months, and she already has $3 million. That's $1 million a month average. Not bad for a beginner." Now, you have to understand that I had been standing in faith every month for money to come in.

Suddenly I could sense those feelings of jealousy trying to get a hold of me, and I had to put them to rest. Sometimes we make excuses for ourselves and judge everyone else. I could have said, "Receiving $3 million after only three months in the ministry could have a negative effect on that girl. She wouldn't have to use her faith to meet her needs. Of course, if it was me, I wouldn't be affected."

I had to put a lid on my negative thoughts. Romans 6:11 says that we are to reckon ourselves "to be dead indeed unto sin," so we need to be dead to jealousy, dead to envy, dead to all those things that try to rise up.

When you are dead to those feelings of jealousy, they don't bother you. You can walk up to someone who is dead and in a casket, and say all kinds of things to them. They are not moved by what they hear. They're dead. You can say, "Man, you are ugly." They're not moved by that.

On the other hand, you could walk up to the corpse and try to puff them up with pride. They are not moved by that either. They're dead. The next time someone tries to get you to step out of love, or offends you, just say, *I'm dead to that.*

The Bible instructs us to rejoice with those who rejoice. (1 Cor. 12:26.) So I made a decision to rejoice with this girl because if it happened to me, I'd be rejoicing.

I promised myself that if I couldn't get the negative feelings under control, I would find out who that girl was and send her an offering. Then she would have $3 million and whatever I gave her. That's how you get back at the devil.

Have you ever believed God for something, such as a new car, and then along comes a new Christian in church? They may have been saved recently, and they dangle a set of car keys and announce, "Look what the Lord has done." Your instincts are to reach out and slap them. We can be tempted, but we don't have to give into it.

One of the great healing evangelists of our time, Kathryn Kuhlman, had many miracles operating in her ministry. People would pop out of wheelchairs like popcorn popping. Some of the media and others used to say and write horrible things about her. People who knew her would say to her, "How could you just ignore that?" But she would reply, "Let's just pretend that it didn't happen." She refused to be offended. When she didn't notice a suffered wrong, as the Bible says, it opened the door for miracles to flow. She walked in love, and God's favor flowed.

God Can Turn It Around

Joseph eventually rose to second in command of Egypt and ran the whole kingdom for Pharaoh. (Gen. 41:40-44.) If the devil has brought something against your life, God can turn it around for good.

But as for you, ye thought evil against me; but God meant it unto good, to bring to pass, as it is this day, to save much people alive.

GENESIS 50:20

Notice he said the people meant it for bad, but God turned it for good. God can turn it around. Something you've experienced, gone through, or maybe you are going through right now, God can become involved in that situation and turn it for good. You can be a blessing. (2 Cor. 1:3,4.)

Maybe you've experienced hurt. You can believe that God will turn your hurt into healing. He can empower you to minister to other hurting people.

Not long ago, I was in a car accident. Someone rear-ended my car on the highway. As soon as it happened, I shouted, "God's going to turn this around. What the devil meant for bad, God will turn for good."

It was a young teenager who hit me. There on the highway I led that kid to the Lord. He was so scared that his dad was going to be really angry with him, so I ministered the love of God to him. I was the nicest person he ever hit. Teenagers are really open to hearing whatever you have to say after smashing up their car and yours. God took a negative situation and turned it into something positive.

Many Channels of Blessing

As a believer, you don't have to limit your income source to your job. God has many ways and avenues of giving you favor and increasing your income. In my life and ministry, on several occasions, I have experienced supernatural favor in finances, even in little areas.

For example, I've received great deals on office equipment, airline tickets, and even a new dress for preaching. Our heavenly Father cares about the small areas of our lives as well.

I realized one day that everywhere I go I experience God's favor. I may be standing in a long line at a store and another line just happens to open up. When shopping, I always seem to find a front-row parking spot and get things on sale. Or a refund check arrives from my insurance company because my rates have gone down unexpectedly.

It's important not to limit God as to how He chooses to bless us. He has many channels and avenues to get provision to us. We must look to Him as our total Source. Your job is just one avenue of blessing. Take the limits off of God and watch His favor work in *every* area of your life.

In the book of Esther, there is a story that wonderfully illustrates the favor of God.

Esther was a beautiful Jewish woman who became queen to King Ahasuerus, although the king was not aware that she was a Jew.

> *The king loved Esther more than all the other women, and she obtained grace and favor in his sight more than all the virgins; so he set the royal crown upon her head and made her queen instead of Vashti.*

> ESTHER 2:17 NKJV

Because of political circumstances in Persia, Esther had to take a stand for her people. Haman, a top advisor to King Ahasuerus, had devised a plan to destroy the entire Jewish nation in Persia, so Esther went before the king on behalf of her people.

In doing so, however, Esther was risking her life. Anyone entering the king's inner court without an invitation could be put to death—unless the king held out his golden scepter to them, signaling his favor.

So it was, when the king saw Queen Esther standing in the court, that she found favor in his sight, and the king held out to Esther the golden scepter that was in his hand....

ESTHER 5:2 NKJV

Repeatedly God granted Esther favor in the king's sight, and the Jewish people were spared.

Just as God granted favor to Esther, He will grant you favor in your life. Whatever you are called to do, God wants to bless *you* with favor.

9

The Influencing Force of Favor

For promotion cometh neither from the east, nor from the west, nor from the south.

But God is the judge: he putteth down one, and setteth up another.

PSALM 75:6,7

9

The Influencing Force of Favor

I began acting on the Word of God early in my Christian walk and confessed Scriptures about the favor of God daily. When God called me to preach at age sixteen, He showed me His plan for my life—I would be teaching and preaching the Gospel throughout America and in other nations. I wondered how this could come to pass—I didn't know even one pastor.

When God called me, He said (in my heart) that I didn't have to wait until I was thirty years old. I was to begin preaching the Gospel while I was young. Some think that when you are young, single, and a woman, the odds are against you. When you have the favor of God, that is not the case. Doors began to open supernaturally as His favor went to work on my behalf.

It is important to remember that promotion does not come from man but from God. (Ps. 75:6,7.) When the call of God is on your life, you never have to prove that you are anointed. Nor do you have to strive to get doors open. Doors of opportunity open when we claim God's favor and allow Him to do the promoting.

In Colossians 4:3 Paul prayed that a door of utterance would be opened to him. Before I ever started preaching, I believed and confessed God's favor daily. I looked at my empty calendar and said, "One day you will be too small to hold all the places that God will send me." And now that has happened!

I constantly confess that I have favor with pastors and their spouses and that God is adding financial partners to my ministry daily so that I can accomplish all He has called me to do. And I *have* favor.

When I was eighteen years old, I went to a service at a rather large church as a visitor. I had spoken to this pastor a few times but only casually. As he walked up to the pulpit that night to preach his message, he said, "There is a special guest here named Kate, and the Holy Spirit wants her to preach tonight."

I was shocked, because he was not the type of pastor to allow someone to preach from his pulpit unless he was very familiar with their ministry. I looked around to see if there was another person in the church named Kate. But the pastor pointed to me and said, "There she is. Come on up here, Kate, and minister the Word of God." The Holy Spirit moved powerfully in that service as I watched God's divine favor in operation. Afterwards, people in his congregation told me the pastor had never invited someone out of the crowd to preach like that before.

Favor With Church Members

Pastors can eliminate many problems in their churches by claiming favor with the people in their congregations.

Please do not misunderstand. I'm not saying this is the solution to every problem in a church. However, because you do have favor, your confession of faith should be that your congregation members are soul winners, tithers, and blessings to your community.

I know a pastor who began to confess that his people were committed and excited about the work of the Lord. One day a guest minister at his church felt led to pray for people who worked in the nursery, children's church, cleaning, and other areas. To the guest minister's surprise, 80 percent of that congregation stood to receive prayer as active workers. The guest minister had never seen such commitment.

That pastor has great favor with the people in his church because he believes for and confesses favor over his congregation daily.

Favor for Souls

The Bible tells us in 2 Corinthians 5:18 that we, as believers, have all been entrusted with "the ministry of reconciliation." This means that God has given each of us the privilege and responsibility of telling others the Good News that Jesus saves.

Psalm 2:8 declares that God will give us lost souls for our inheritance when we ask Him. We all need to begin to exercise our faith for winning the lost. We can have favor with people who don't know Jesus. And because we have favor with lost people, they will get saved in our meetings.

Before I go to minister, I thank the Lord that I have so much favor with the lost that they come to hear my message and that they will receive my message and be saved. We *do* have favor with the lost. And the angels, who are "ministering spirits, sent forth to minister for them who shall be heirs of salvation" (Heb. 1:14), will help us as we minister to people with the invitation to receive salvation.

In the book of Acts, thousands of souls were added to the church daily. They gathered from long distances and from the surrounding areas as the Good News of salvation was preached. You, too, can share the Gospel with great favor.

I want to encourage you to begin to believe God for favor with lost people. One of the reasons so many people get saved in my meetings is that I confess that when lost people come, I will have favor with them.

You, too, can claim favor with lost people. Believe that you'll have supernatural favor with them and that they'll want to hear what you're saying. They *will* be interested in what you have to say, especially when you claim favor with them.

Favor for Fun

You should expect God to do radical things for you. He wants to bless you with favor, even in the little areas of your life.

For example, I really liked the old television show *Dr. Quinn, Medicine Woman.* One time when it was still on the air, I was preaching in California. While I was there, I thought,

Lord, I'd really like to meet Dr. Quinn—Jane Seymour. Can you believe I asked God for something like that?

If your life is boring, ask God for anything fun. He wants to bless your life. Some people say, "Oh, I wouldn't ask God for that." Well, that may be why you're bored, and I'm having fun. Many times we have not because we ask not. (James 4:2.)

When I finished preaching, a young man I had gone to Bible school with approached me. He said, "I don't know if you know this or not, Kate, but I've been acting on some television shows. I play as an extra on *Dr. Quinn.* Have you ever heard of that show?"

I said, "Of course, I have. It's funny that you should ask."

He said, "Would you like to come out to the set? I can show you around. Would something like that interest you?"

I didn't tell him I had prayed about that situation. I answered quickly, "I would love to."

He cautioned me, "Jane Seymour is probably not going to be there because…."

I answered, "She'll be there."

He asked, "How do you know?"

I said, "I just know."

Then he said, "She might be busy doing different things; you probably won't get to…."

I said, "I'll meet her."

Again, he asked, "How do you know?"

I said, "I've got favor; just hide and watch."

So we arrived, and I had so much favor that I got to see every inch of the set.

As we approached the famous house used on the show, my friend said, "We probably won't get in. They always keep the door locked."

"*I know it's unlocked,*" I thought. "*God, You set this day up just for me.*" The door was unlocked, and I was able to go in and see everything.

As it turned out, Jane Seymour *was* working that day. My friend left to go take care of something, and as I was sitting there alone minding my own business, Jane Seymour came out a door right next to me. She was just standing there waiting between scenes, and she said hello to me. So I said hello back, and we started talking! We talked about all kinds of things. She asked me why I was in California and that opened the door to share the Gospel with her.

When my friend came back, he couldn't believe that I was standing there talking with Jane Seymour like we were old buddies! What a fun day that was. Later, I met several Christians who worked on the set of *Dr. Quinn,* and they held a Bible study. They asked me if I would return and preach for them. God is so good! He will even give you favor in areas that seem trivial to some folks but really bless you.

10

Twenty Ways You
Can Lose Your Favor

A good man out of the good treasure of his heart bringeth forth that which is good; and an evil man out of the evil treasure of his heart bringeth forth that which is evil: for of the abundance of the heart his mouth speaketh.

LUKE 6:45

10

Twenty Ways You Can Lose Your Favor

Here are some reasons why people sometimes do not receive favor. It could be that you're in the wrong place, such as the wrong job.

I remember how one time I wanted a particular job so badly that I prayed for favor, and I finally got the job. I soon discovered that I didn't like the job, and the Lord showed me it was not where He wanted me to be. It was where I wanted to be. I pushed and pushed so hard for this job I think God finally just said, "Okay, you can have it, but it's not My best."

That is similar to the time Israel continued to ask God for a king. (1 Sam. 8:6,19.) He didn't want them to have a king, but He gave them one anyway because they kept bugging Him. You see, He wanted to be their King instead. It would have been better God's way, because the king they got turned out to be a mess.

It's important to hear God's voice and be where He wants you to be. Often people push for favor in areas without checking first with God to see if that's where He wants them.

We Must Do Our Part

A lot of times people are praying for favor, but they are not giving it their absolute best. For example, some people are constantly late for work and claim favor for a raise. That's just not going to work. If you are frequently late for work, you can't expect favor with your boss. You must do your part.

We have a responsibility to live as God teaches us to live and treat others well. Do the absolute best job you can do. Be a person of excellence. That in itself will help bring favor to your life.

You must be practical. For example, a Bible school student had read how angels provide protection so he left his kids at home alone. Angels will not baby-sit. We have some responsibility to do our part. We can't do a lousy job at work, always be late, create problems, not be submissive, and expect favor.

Here are twenty ways you can stop the flow of God's favor in your life.

In General

1. Don't keep your word.

    God expects honor and integrity. (1 Chron. 29:17; Matt. 5:37.) When you make a commitment, keep your word.

Place high value on what comes out of your mouth. God does.

2. Be rude and pushy.

Choose to love above all other things. God told us to love one another. (John 13:34.) Exhibit the characteristics of love found in 1 Corinthians 13.

3. Have a negative attitude.

The Bible tells us that a merry heart does us good, like a medicine (Prov. 17:22), and that the joy of the Lord is our strength. (Neh. 8:10.) It is in us, and we should overflow with joy—eliminating negative attitudes.

4. Dress and groom yourself poorly.

We are instructed to present ourselves a living sacrifice, holy and "acceptable unto God." (Rom. 12:1.) Be proud of who you are in Christ. You are a child of the Most High God. Your appearance and grooming reflect what you think about yourself. Represent God and yourself well.

At Work

6. Always be late/always leave early.

Your work is not "just a job." You are sowing into what belongs to another person. The Bible says to be faithful to that which is another man's, and God will give you your own. (Luke 16:12.) You can't be late, leave early, and claim favor.

7. Use work time for soul winning.

Conduct yourself as a person of integrity. If you are "on the clock," so to speak, then spend that time working. What I mean by this is that you are being paid to work, not witness. When you are preaching on your employer's time, without their permission, you are stealing from them. It would be better to do an awesome job and share Jesus on your time, not their time.

8. Complain about your boss.

Honor those you work for. Support them with your words, deeds, and prayers. Don't be a complainer. If you complain, you will remain.

9. Have a negative attitude.

Luke 6:45 NKJV says, "For out of the abundance of the heart his mouth speaks." If you profess to be a Christian, you should be more positive than negative. Live your life as a walking witness of God's goodness.

At Church

10. Don't pay your tithe.

Malachi 3:10 instructs us to bring all the tithes into the storehouse. Our tithe is 10 percent of our increase. Give back to God the portion that belongs to Him, and He will bless you.

11. Gossip about the pastor.

    Have you ever had roast pastor for lunch? I hope not. That means you gossip about him over lunch. Speak faith-filled words over your pastor and church.

12. Murmur about how things are done.

    "… for the Lord hears your complaints which you make against Him. And what are we? Your complaints are not against us but against the Lord" (Ex. 16:8 NKJV). The children of Israel could not enter into the Promised Land because they murmured. They wandered around for forty years, when it would have only taken them eleven days.

13. Don't follow through with commitments.

    Again, keep your word. Really think it through before you make a commitment, so you can keep your word. Be honest if you can't do something. Only commit if you will follow through.

14. Insist on your own way.

    By insisting on your own way, you can lose your favor. Instead, put others before yourself. That's walking in love.

In Relationships

15. Be ungrateful.

    Thankfulness has power. We are to give thanks with a grateful heart. (Ps. 66:8 AMP; 1 Cor. 2:9 AMP.) Rejoice in what God and others have done for you, and let them know by telling them so.

16. Take people for granted.

God has given you gifts—the people in your life. Treat them as such. (Prov. 27:17.)

17. Always think of yourself first.

How do we do this? By being selfish. (Phil. 2:3 NKJV.)

18. Hold a grudge.

Don't stop the flow of favor in your life by holding a grudge. When someone offends you, don't nurse it, don't rehearse it, but curse it, disburse it, and God will reverse it. Let it go, and stay free to receive favor in your life.

At School

19. Don't study or do your homework.

Second Timothy 2:15 says, "Study to shew thyself approved unto God...."

20. Be a smart aleck.

Avoid a haughty look, a proud, sharp tongue. (Prov. 18:12.)

21. Don't obey the rules.

Obedience brings blessing. (Deut. 28:1-13.)

Kate's Quotes

- One day of favor is worth a thousand days of labor.
- God will turn your test into a testimony.

- God will turn your mess into a message of victory.
- When someone offends you, don't nurse it, don't rehearse it; curse it, disburse it, and God will reverse it.
- You can be bitter or you can better, but you can't be bitter and better at the same time.
- The "FOG" is rolling in: Favor of God.
- Joseph went from the pit to the palace in twenty-four hours, and so can you!
- God can turn your hurt into healing.
- God's favor can save you hours of labor.
- God says, "Give me your will, and I will show you My ways." Satan says, "Give me your will, and I'll have my way."
- There's always Someone watching you who's capable of greatly blessing you.

Testimonies of Favor

Oh that men would praise the Lord for his goodness, and for his wonderful works to the children of men!

PSALM 107:8

Testimonies of Favor

The following are testimonies from those who applied principles from *The Blessing of Favor:*

Dear Kate,

Thank you for writing your book on favor. I read it today, and my life is changed. I believe I receive and have the favor of God upon my life. I attract all favor!

As I was reading the truth of the Word, it shattered through feelings of rejection. The Father, through His Spirit, answered some "why" questions I had been asking. It was too good. Even while I sat reading your book, I was hungry. Guess what? A saint came to me and offered me a peanut butter sandwich. Of course, I said yes! Favor!

The part [in the book] about unforgiveness stopping favor was so powerful. This is where the Spirit spoke to my heart about unforgiveness because of rejection from others, which only led to bitterness [in my life]. Much of it was my fault because I thought I deserved to be overlooked. Not anymore. God's favor surrounds me like a shield. Even when I do make mistakes, I have favor in the sight of God and man.

I plan to keep a "favor" journal starting today with the peanut butter sandwich.

—C.M., Tuskegee, Alabama

Dear Kate,

I read your book, and you talked about how this man's boss gave him a raise, and he was making more than his boss was. I had confessed with my mouth that I was going to get a raise and began praising [God]. Well, I had forgotten about my confession, but two weeks ago my boss called me in her office, and she said that I was doing a good job. She said she really appreciated me and that I was going to get a raise—and I did. Praise the Lord. I can see a difference in my check.

—S.D., Tulsa, Oklahoma

Dear Kate,

My husband bought your book for me as an anniversary gift. I read the book about a week later. During my quiet time one morning I saw your book on my table and decided that if God could grant you favor, He could do the same for me. I then recited several of the Scriptures on favor that are in the back of the book. I especially took notice and said Psalm 5:12 and Psalm 90:17. I went to work and not 30 minutes after I was at work my boss asked me to come to his office. He told me I would be getting a raise on my next paycheck. I was stunned at first, but later, I remembered the Scriptures I had recited earlier. I thanked God for His favor!

—D.S., Mount Pleasant, Iowa

Dear Kate,

I bought your book and have been blessed. I prayed and asked God to give me favor with my boss. I went on vacation, and I wanted to be off one more day so my vacation wouldn't be split up. I called and asked if I could have one more day off. Praise the Lord, [my boss] said yes! Now I have another week off. I am so excited. Usually when I asked for certain days off after the schedule was made, [my boss] would always say no. Praise the Lord.

—S.D., Tulsa, Oklahoma

Dear Kate,

I love your book because it works!

—P.P.

Dear Kate,

Your book blessed us so. My son went to public school until this year. He is in the second grade. We put him in a Christian school. At night when we pray, he and I and my four-year-old confess that we have the mind of Christ, that the mighty Holy Spirit lives on the inside of us and helps us to learn quickly. His life and His knowledge are in us today. When [my son] started the second grade, he couldn't read. I had a talk with his teacher yesterday, and in one semester, he has caught up. Although some things are more of a challenge, he is doing them. Hallelujah! Thank you for your book.

—P.M.

Dear Kate,

A friend I work with bought [your book on favor], and I couldn't put it down until I was finished. I have been in a walk with the Lord before, but He has shown me many things I never realized before. I feel like a person walking out of a dimly lit room into a big, bright, beautifully lit room! Thank you so much for writing your book. It has shown me so many new things, and I feel God placed this book here for me to read and understand.

S.H., Smithville, Indiana

Prayers for Favor

Daily Prayer for Favor

Father, thank You for making me righteous through the blood of Jesus. Because of that I am blessed and Your favor surrounds me as a shield. When I talk with people, the first thing they come into contact with is my favor shield.

Thank You that I have favor with You and man today. All day long people go out of their way to bless and help me. I have favor with everyone I deal with today.

I am increasing in wisdom and favor today. I am more than a conqueror in every situation that comes my way.

Because of Your favor upon my life, Lord, I am a delight to people. They enjoy me and take pleasure in being around me. Your willingness and grace make me pleasing and acceptable to everyone I meet today.

Thank You, Father, that You are in me and with me everywhere I go today so that I am delivered out of every distress and affliction. Everyone I meet sees that I have goodwill, favor, wisdom, and understanding because of Your Spirit living in me. In Jesus' name, amen.

Scripture References

Romans 5:9

2 Corinthians 5:21

Psalm 5:12

2 Corinthians 6:16 AMP

Luke 2:52

Romans 8:37

Proverbs 3:3,4

Favor in Relationships

Father, I thank You for blessing me with good, healthy relationships. I ask You to send me the kind of friends You want me to have. I thank You that Your favor is attracting godly relationships—relationships that will help challenge me spiritually and draw me into a deeper walk with You. Supernaturally remove me from any relationship that would be harmful or would not glorify You.

I ask You, Lord, to give me wisdom in relationships. Help me to be a good friend, one who is led and guided by Your Spirit.

I pray for all of my family relationships. I bind strife and division between me and any family member, and I loose peace and harmony between us. I declare that the enemy is not allowed to cause strife in my family in any way, shape, or form. As for me and my house, we will serve You, Lord. I speak that all of my family is saved, and we walk in love toward each other. In Jesus' name, amen.

Scripture References

Proverbs 18:24

Proverbs 27:17

2 Corinthians 6:14

James 1:5

James 3:16,17

Matthew 18:18

Joshua 24:15

Acts 16:31

Favor in Marriage

Father, I will sow love, patience, and kindness toward _____(name of spouse) today, and therefore, I have favor with them. I am never jealous of them or their time. I am not rude to _____; I always treat them with respect. I don't insist on having my own way, and I'm not touchy or resentful toward _____. I don't keep track of, or even pay attention to, things they do wrong. I'm happy when things go well, when right and truth prevail. My love for _____ bears up under anything and everything that comes, and I always believe the best of them. My hopes for _____ never fade, and my love for _____ never fails.

I purpose to walk in love with _____. I esteem, love, and delight in _____, just as Christ loves me.

Father, thank You that _____ and I are kind and affectionate with each other. I put _____ first and honor _____ before myself, and because of Your favor, _____ does the same with me.

Our marriage is flourishing and our prayers are not hindered, because _____ and I walk in love. We are joint heirs of Your unmerited favor. We are united in spirit, and we love each other. We are compassionate, courteous, tenderhearted, and humble-minded toward each other. We never return evil for evil or insult for insult. We never scold each other or put each other down, but we bless each other, praying for each other's welfare, happiness, and protection.

_____ and I have favor with You and man; people go out of their way to bless us and our family. In Jesus' name, amen.

Scripture References

Galatians 6:7

1 Corinthians 13:4,8 AMP

Ephesians 5:2 AMP

1 Peter 3:7-9 AMP

Romans 12:10

Romans 8:17

Proverbs 3:3,4

Favor on the Job

Father, I thank You that promotion doesn't come from the east or the west or the south but from You. Because of Your favor upon me, I will be lifted up and promoted at my job.

Just as You were with Joseph, Lord, so You are with me on my job. Thank You for showing me mercy and lovingkindness and for giving me favor with everyone I come in contact with today, especially my superiors. Thank You for making whatever I do prosper.

Father, I purpose in my heart to be diligent. I am giving my all at what I do for a living, and people are noticing. The world may think that education, brilliance, or being well connected "maketh rich," but even though those things can be helpful, I thank You that Your Word says, "...the hand of the *diligent* maketh rich." Because of You, my superiors like me and favor me. In Jesus' name, amen.

Scripture References

Psalm 75:6,7   Proverbs 10:4

Genesis 39:21-23 AMP

Favor at School

Father, I thank You that I have supernatural favor with my teachers and classmates. I ask You for wisdom, and I believe I am growing in it. Thank You that I have the mind of Christ.

The mighty Holy Spirit lives on the inside of me and helps me to learn quickly. His life and knowledge are in me today.

I can do all things through Christ who strengthens me. Because of Your favor, Lord, if there's an award to win, I can win it. If there's a scholarship available, it is for me. I am more than a conqueror in You, Lord. In Jesus' name, amen.

Scripture References

Psalm 5:12

Luke 2:52

1 Corinthians 2:16

1 John 4:4 AMP

Philippians 4:13

Romans 8:37

Favor in Ministry/ Winning the Lost

Father, I thank You for divine favor that supernaturally opens doors of opportunity for me to preach the Gospel, to proclaim the mystery concerning Christ the Messiah. Your favor is working on my behalf, and I do not have to strive in the flesh to get doors to open.

Jesus Christ has reconciled me to You, Father, and given me the ministry of reconciliation. I have favor when I talk to people about You, Lord; they listen to everything I say and are eager to receive You as their Savior.

Father, I ask You to give me the lost people of this world for my inheritance. Thank You that I have favor when I go preach to them.

You are working through me to bring many souls into Your kingdom. You, Father, give me favor and goodwill with all people so that I can preach the Good News of Jesus to them, and they can be added to Your kingdom. In Jesus' name, amen.

Scripture References

Colossians 4:3 AMP   Psalm 2:8

2 Corinthians 5:18,19   Acts 2:47 AMP

Overcoming Hindrances to Favor

Unforgiveness

I purpose to forgive. Because I forgive them, You forgive me, Father, and my prayers are not hindered.

I am bought with a price, the precious blood of Jesus Christ. Therefore, my life is not my own, and I choose Your will over my own, Lord. I'm not directed by my feelings. I cast down thoughts of bitterness and choose to walk in love.

Lord, I ask You to bless them in every way today; I pray for their welfare, happiness and protection. I let go of the wrong that has been committed against me. I give up any resentment that I feel toward them. I release them and forgive them. I thank You for Your love, forgiveness, and favor, Lord. In Jesus' name, amen.

Scripture References

Mark 11:25,26

1 Corinthians 6:20

Matthew 6:12-15 AMP

1 Peter 3:9 AMP

Luke 6:37 AMP

Luke 11:4

Matthew 5:44

Negative Thinking

I see myself as You see me, Father. I am unconditionally loved and accepted because of the blood Jesus shed for me. I refuse to think thoughts of inferiority and rejection. I have favor with You, Father, and with man, so people treat me well all day long.

I cast down every imagination or picture of myself as insecure, because that is not how You truly see me, Lord. I only think on those things that are obedient and pleasing to You, Lord Jesus—things that are lovely and kind and worthy of praise.

You created and care for me, Father. You have crowned me with glory and honor. Because I am Your child, Your Word says that I have the same glory that You gave to Jesus and that I am one with Him.

I am more than a conqueror through Christ. I am loved completely, totally, and unconditionally by the Creator of the universe. You accept me, Father, and I am righteous in Your Son, Jesus Christ. In Jesus' name, amen.

Scripture References

John 3:16	2 Corinthians 10:5
Ephesians 2:4	Psalm 8:4,5
Philippians 4:8 AMP	John 17:22 AMP
Ephesians 1:6	Romans 8:37

Scriptures on Favor

Scriptures on Favor

For thou, Lord, wilt bless the righteous; with favour wilt thou compass him as with a shield.

PSALM 5:12

Let not mercy and truth forsake thee: bind them about thy neck; write them upon the table of thine heart:

So shalt thou find favour and good understanding in the sight of God and man.

PROVERBS 3:3,4

"Glory to God in the highest, and on earth peace to men on whom his favor rests."

LUKE 2:14 NIV

For he says, "In the time of my favor I heard you, and in the day of salvation I helped you." I tell you, now is the time of God's favor, now is the day of salvation.

2 CORINTHIANS 6:2 NIV

May the favor of the Lord our God rest upon us; establish the work of our hands for us—yes, establish the work of our hands.

PSALM 90:17 NIV

For the Lord God is a sun and shield; the Lord bestows favor and honor; no good thing does he withhold from those whose walk is blameless.

PSALM 84:11 NIV

Good understanding wins favor, but the way of the unfaithful is hard.

PROVERBS 13:15 NIV

He becometh poor that dealeth with a slack hand: but the hand of the diligent maketh rich.

PROVERBS 10:4

For whoever finds me [wisdom] finds life and receives favor from the Lord.

PROVERBS 8:35 NIV

Obey them [your masters] not only to win their favor when their eye is on you, but like slaves of Christ, doing the will of God from your heart.

EPHESIANS 6:6 NIV

Slaves, obey your earthly masters in everything; and do it, not only when their eye is on you and to win their favor, but with sincerity of heart and reverence for the Lord.

COLOSSIANS 3:22 NIV

For promotion cometh neither from the east, nor from the west, nor from the south.

But God is the judge: he putteth down one, and setteth up another.

PSALM 75:6,7

Knowing that whatsoever good thing any man doeth, the same shall he receive of the Lord, whether he be bond or free.

EPHESIANS 6:8

Bless the Lord, O my soul, and forget not all his benefits:

Who forgiveth all thine iniquities; who healeth all thy diseases;

Who redeemeth thy life from destruction; who crowneth thee with lovingkindness and tender mercies.

PSALM 103:2-4

Nay, in all these things we are more than conquerors through him that loved us.

ROMANS 8:37

For God so loved the world, that he gave his only begotten Son, that whosoever believeth in him should not perish, but have everlasting life.

JOHN 3:16

But God, who is rich in mercy, for his great love wherewith he loved us.

EPHESIANS 2:4

To the praise of the glory of his grace, wherein he hath made us accepted in the beloved.

EPHESIANS 1:6

Much more then, being now justified by his blood, we shall be saved from wrath through him.

ROMANS 5:9

For he hath made him to be sin for us, who knew no sin; that we might be made the righteousness of God in him.

2 CORINTHIANS 5:21

Ye are of God, little children, and have overcome them: because greater is he that is in you, than he that is in the world.

1 JOHN 4:4

Verily I say unto you, Whatsoever ye shall bind on earth shall be bound in heaven: and whatsoever ye shall loose on earth shall be loosed in heaven.

Again I say unto you, That if two of you shall agree on earth as touching any thing that they shall ask, it shall be done for them of my Father which is in heaven.

MATTHEW 18:18,19

And when ye stand praying, forgive, if ye have ought against any: that your Father also which is in heaven may forgive you your trespasses.

MARK 11:25

Judge not, and ye shall not be judged: condemn not, and ye shall not be condemned: forgive, and ye shall be forgiven.

LUKE 6:37

But I say unto you, Love your enemies, bless them that curse you, do good to them that hate you, and pray for them which despitefully use you, and persecute you.

MATTHEW 5:44

Not rendering evil for evil, or railing for railing: but contrariwise blessing; knowing that ye are thereunto called, that ye should inherit a blessing.

1 PETER 3:9

Ask of me, and I shall give thee the heathen for thine inheritance, and the uttermost parts of the earth for thy possession.

PSALM 2:8

And they said, Believe on the Lord Jesus Christ, and thou shalt be saved, and thy house.

ACTS 16:31

But all things are from God, Who through Jesus Christ reconciled us to Himself [received us into favor, brought us into harmony with Himself] and gave to us the ministry of reconciliation [that by word and deed we might aim to bring others into harmony with Him].

It was God [personally present] in Christ, reconciling and restoring the world to favor with Himself, not counting up and holding against [men] their trespasses [but canceling them], and committing to us the message of reconciliation (of the restoration to favor).

2 CORINTHIANS 5:18,19 AMP

And Jesus increased in wisdom and stature, and in favour with God and man.

LUKE 2:52

Praising God, and having favour with all the people. And the Lord added to the church daily such as should be saved.

ACTS 2:47

But the Lord was with Joseph, and shewed him mercy, and gave him favour in the sight of the keeper of the prison.

And the keeper of the prison committed to Joseph's hand all the prisoners that were in the prison; and whatsoever they did there, he was the doer of it.

The keeper of the prison looked not to any thing that was under his hand; because the Lord was with him, and that which he did, the Lord made it to prosper.

GENESIS 39:21-23

And the patriarchs, moved with envy, sold Joseph into Egypt: but God was with him,

And delivered him out of all his afflictions, and gave him favour and wisdom in the sight of Pharaoh king of Egypt; and he made him governor over Egypt and all his house.

ACTS 7:9,10

My Favor Journal

There's power in writing things down. Habakkuk 2:2 says, "…Write the vision, and make it plain upon tables, that he may run that readeth it." I encourage you to keep a journal of the favor of God as it manifests in your life, from the smallest little incident to the biggest exciting thing. Remember, the more you acknowledge God's favor, the more you will receive. You'll be amazed to look back and see everything that God's favor has done.

My Favor Journal

Date_____

Confession/Scripture: _____

_____

_____

_____

_____

_____

_____

Favor acknowledged in my life today: _____

_____

_____

_____

_____

_____

_____

_____

_____

_____

Special notes to myself: _____

_____

_____

_____

_____

_____

_____

My Favor Journal

Date_____

Confession/Scripture: _____

_____

_____

_____

_____

_____

_____

Favor acknowledged in my life today: _____

_____

_____

_____

_____

_____

_____

_____

_____

_____

Special notes to myself: _____

_____

_____

_____

_____

_____

_____

My Favor Journal

Date_____

Confession/Scripture: _____

_____

_____

_____

_____

_____

_____

Favor acknowledged in my life today: _____

_____

_____

_____

_____

_____

_____

_____

_____

_____

Special notes to myself: _____

_____

_____

_____

_____

_____

My Favor Journal

Date_____

Confession/Scripture: _____

_____

_____

_____

_____

_____

_____

Favor acknowledged in my life today: _____

_____

_____

_____

_____

_____

_____

_____

_____

_____

Special notes to myself: _____

_____

_____

_____

_____

_____

_____

My Favor Journal

Date_____

Confession/Scripture: _____

_____

_____

_____

_____

_____

_____

Favor acknowledged in my life today: _____

_____

_____

_____

_____

_____

_____

_____

_____

_____

Special notes to myself: _____

_____

_____

_____

_____

_____

_____

Endnotes

Chapter 2

[1] *Webster's New World College Dictionary,* 3d ed. (New York: Simon & Shuster, Inc., copyright 1997, 1996, 1994, 1991, 1988), s.v. "favor."

[2] Ibid., "favored."

Chapter 3

[1] *American Dictionary of the English Language,* 10th ed. (San Francisco: Foundation for American Christian Education, 1998). Facsimile of Noah Webster's 1828 edition, permission to reprint by G. & C. Merriam Company, copyright 1967 & 1995 (Renewal) by Rosalie J. Slater, s.v. "REDEEMED."

[2] Webster's, s.v. "redeem."

Chapter 4

[1] Based upon a definition in Webster's, s.v. "increase."

[2] W. E. Vine, *Expository Dictionary of New Testament Words* (Old Tappan, New Jersey: Fleming H. Revell Company, 1966), p. 163, s.v. "CALL, CALLED, CALLING, A. Verbs, No. 1, KALEO."

Chapter 6

[1] Based upon a definition in Webster's, s.v. "man."

Chapter 7

[1] Based upon a definition in Noah Webster's 1828 edition, s.v. "ANOINT."

An Important Message

If you have never met Jesus Christ, you can know Him today. God cares for you and wants to help you in every area of your life. That is why He sent Jesus to die for you. You can make your life right with God this very moment and make heaven your home.

Pray this prayer now:

Oh, God, I ask You to forgive me of my sins. I believe You sent Jesus to die on the cross for me. I receive Jesus Christ as my personal Lord and Savior. I confess Him as Lord of my life, and I give my life to Him. Thank You, Lord, for saving me and for making me new. In Jesus' name, amen.

If you prayed this prayer, I welcome you to the family of God.

Please write to the address that follows and let me know about your decision for Jesus. I want to send you some free literature to help you in your new walk with the Lord.

To contact Kate McVeigh for book, tape, or ministry information, or for prayer, write:

Kate McVeigh Ministries

P. O. Box 1688 • Warren, Michigan 48090

Or call: 1-800-40-FAITH (1-800-403-2484)

Or visit our Web site: www.katemcveigh.org

About the Author

Rev. Kate McVeigh ministers extensively throughout the United States and abroad, preaching the Gospel of Jesus Christ with signs and wonders following. Her outreach ministry includes books, teaching tapes, daily radio broadcast "The Voice of Faith," as well as her weekly television broadcast, which airs throughout the United States.

Kate is known as a solid evangelist and teacher of the Gospel, with a powerful anointing to heal the sick and win the lost. Through Kate's down-to-earth and often humorous teaching of the Word, many are motivated to attain God's best for their lives.

Additional copies of this book
are available from your local bookstore.

Harrison House
Tulsa, Oklahoma 74153

The Harrison House Vision

Proclaiming the truth and the power
Of the Gospel of Jesus Christ
With excellence;

Challenging Christians to
Live victoriously,
Grow spiritually,
Know God intimately.